MOTHER DEATH

Mother Death

The Journal of Jules Michelet

1815–1850

Translated and edited by

Edward K. Kaplan

The University of Massachusetts Press
Amherst, 1984

Frontispiece:
Portrait de Jules Michelet by Thomas Couture.
Musée Carnavalet (GIRAUDON)

Printed in the United States of America

Library of Congress Cataloging in Publication Data
Michelet, Jules, 1798–1874.
Mother death.
Translated selections from: Écrits de jeunesse,
Journal, and La montagne.
Bibliography: p.
Includes index.
1. Michelet, Jules, 1798–1874. 2. Historians—
France—Biography. 3. Bereavement. I. Kaplan, Edward K.,
1942. II. Title.
DC36.98.M5A25 1984 944'.0072024 [B] 83–18068
ISBN 0–87023–432–3

To My Parents

KIVIE KAPLAN
(1 April 1904–5 May 1975)

EMILY ROGERS KAPLAN
(19 March 1905–26 January 1981)

Of Blessed Memory

Acknowledgments

Every Michelet reader stands on the shoulders of Paul Viallaneix, editor of three volumes of the *Journal* and editor-in-chief of the *Oeuvres complètes* now in production at Flammarion. I am especially grateful for his personal and professional support over the years, for permission to quote his editions of the *Journal*, and for his Chronology, first published in *La Voie royale* (1959), modified for the purposes of this book. My special appreciation to Oscar A. Haac, author of the best introduction to Michelet in French or in English, and to the psychohistorian Rudolph Binion for their painstaking reading of a previous version of the manuscript. Benjamin F. Bart, Stephen J. Gendzier, Frank E. Manuel, Avery D. Weisman, and Seymour Weiner also offered valuable suggestions for improvement. Tracy Cooke and Sara Horowitz helped with the initial stages of the translation, and Jean Albert Rousseau translated Michelet's Greek and Latin quotations. Judith Stark and Erica Goldberg typed the manuscript in a way that inspired confidence. Yuan Zhou helped prepare the index.

Also contributing significantly were Michael and Mona Fishbane, Alexandra G. Kaplan, Bonnie P. Marxer, Robert E. Meagher, Albert J. Salvan, Sandi Slone, Francis Steegmuller, and my colleagues in Shiffman Hall. Brandeis University provided a stimulating and congenial place to work, talk, and think, and financial support.

My son, Jeremy Joshua Kaplan, constantly reminded me what life is truly about, while the memory of several deceased friends also companioned my work on these pages: S. Ralph Harlow (20 July 1885–21 August 1972), Abraham Joshua Heschel (11 January 1907–23 December 1972), Albert Ougeile (14 November 1919–3 August 1975), Howard Thurman (18 November 1900–10 April 1981), and my parents, Emily and Kivie Kaplan, to whom this volume is dedicated.

Contents

Preface

Most English-speaking readers first encountered Michelet in the opening chapters of Edmund Wilson's groundbreaking "study in the writing and acting of history," *To the Finland Station* (1940). The American critic surveyed the sweep of the Romantic historian's encyclopedic interests and successfully captured his passionate identification with the French revolutionary tradition. I first discovered Michelet, quite by chance, in the French philosopher Gaston Bachelard's exploration of poetic imagination, *Water and Dreams* (1942), which presented the historian as a dreamer of presurrealistic originality in touch with his deepest impulses. Bachelard quoted oddly fascinating passages from two of Michelet's lyrical popularizations of science, *The Sea* (1861) and *The Mountain* (1868), in which seawater and mud carried powerful maternal associations. Then I read Roland Barthes's 1954 book on Michelet which, inspired by Bachelard, revealed the historian as an extraordinary stylist, obsessed with death and excited by the violence and urgency of time and events. For modern readers of literature and history, Michelet exemplifies the drama of writing itself.

Jules Michelet (1798–1874) provides rich pasture for several contemporary concerns. Roland Barthes used Michelet to probe the psychoanalytical unconscious of literature. He studied the historian's imagery and delineated networks of subjective associations that appeared to condition his ideology. Psychohistorians, or students of the creative process in general, can learn much from Michelet's frequent narrative interventions, his practice of history as autobiography, and from his private *Journal*—not published until 1959. His personal and published writings allow us to participate in the religious, political, and scientific debates of his era—the Romantic period during which science competed with fantasy among poets and social thinkers alike. Everything he has written, in fact, reveals a tender and tumultuous inner life.

Michelet has dominated the first fifteen years of my academic career.

As a doctoral candidate, directed by Michael Riffaterre, I began in 1967 to study his nonhistorical works—volumes on nature, the working classes, education, women and marriage, witchcraft, and world religions. These works of popular education applied the historian's ideology to the France of his day. I expanded my dissertation into a book, *Michelet's Poetic Vision: A Romantic Philosophy of Nature, Man, and Woman* (1977), in which I analyzed the mythical system that came to full expression during the second half of his career. The mature writer elaborated a philosophical alternative to Christianity that linked nature and mankind, male and female, in a universal thrust toward freedom and, ultimately, a spiritual existence beyond the grave. His pre-Darwinian theory of nature's evolution completed his philosophy of mankind. He imagined that animals, people, and even minerals possessed a free will, part of the divine force.

Michelet's life was as rich and complex as his thoughts. While writing the book, I had also undertaken a detailed investigation of his day-to-day existence, his readings, and his methods of composition. I examined his unpublished correspondence, drafts and finished manuscripts, as well as his diaries. The goal was to establish a critical edition of his first two books on nature, *L'Oiseau* and *L'Insecte*. These poetic essays, which mix research and reverie, throb with the author's obsession with death. *The Bird* (1856) celebrated the creative powers of the nightingale, an image of the poet; while *The Insect* (1857), through the analogy of metamorphosis, would prove that an angelic soul emerges from the flesh, as a butterfly from the earthbound cocoon. He sought to "demonstrate that death does not exist."[1]

Michelet continued to captivate me after the critical editions went to press following ten years of preparation. His superb lyrical prose enthralled me as he brought mankind's great actors back to life through artistic empathy and reproduced the hidden thoughts of birds, ants, bees, and sea creatures. He was truly, as he himself put it, an "artist-historian." Vivid, dramatic images and magnificent rhythmic French gratified my love of poetry, and his lofty democratic hopes inspired my yearning for harmony, grandeur, and peace. But I could not fathom the terror beneath the dream: his ghoulish attraction to death. Miche-

---

1 See below, entry of 20 May 1842.

let was a haunted man. Even while he successfully resurrected the past, his anxiety prevailed.

He could not fully reconcile his public posture with his private doubts. Michelet's philosophy of nature and humanity exemplified the shortcomings as well as the strengths of French Romantic liberalism during the early decades of the nineteenth century. He formed the ideals of 1789 into a middle-class utopia vigorously opposed to authoritarian Christianity. He expected his books to become a non-Christian Bible, and his lectures at the Collège de France, the nation's leading intellectual forum, echoed calls for revolutionary freedom and equality for all. A thousand admirers flocked to his courses during those tumultuous years before the 1848 revolution. The professor and the historian would replace the priest as the nation's moral guide. But his exalted view of the intellectual—the Romantic avatar of the Enlightenment *philosophe*—did not abolish his intimate conflicts.

Michelet's preoccupation with mortality illuminates the mysteries of bereavement and the creative urges often inspired by loss. I returned to study the historian's diaries, the repository of his readings, conversations, ideas, sleeping dreams, and waking reveries. These meticulous and often eloquent self-examinations helped me to penetrate further into the underground, the tensions within the optimistic "vision of nature, man, and woman" examined in my first book. The present one shares my understanding of the man's struggles.

– Forgotten! Dreadful word. How could a soul perish from within other souls!... The person God created for life, does he not enjoy the right to survive, at least within the mind? Who on this earth would dare to inflict, even upon the guiltiest, that death beyond all death: abolish him from memories?
Introduction to *History of the French Revolution*, section 9 (dated 31 January 1847) –

Introduction

– It is a fact that history, in the progress of time, makes the historian much more than it is made by him. My book has created me. It is I who am its handiwork. This son has produced its father. If it first issued from me, from my storm of youth (which still rages), it has rendered me much stronger, more enlightened, even given me more fertile warmth, more actual power to resurrect the past. Preface to *History of France* (1869) –

—"I HAD A NOBLE disease which clouded my youth, yet which well suited an historian. I loved death. I had lived nine years at the doors of the Père-Lachaise cemetery, at that time my only place for walking," Michelet wrote in the 1869 preface to his *History of France.* Recent studies of attitudes toward mortality view current fixations on death as part of a universal drama, but Michelet understood that fear of death was the origin of History itself. One writes about the past in order to retrieve what has perished. No historian has studied his own grief more intently than Jules Michelet, whose ambition was to conquer extinction. He was a literary artist dedicated, as he said, to the "resurrection of the integral life of the past."

His teaching and writing were apostolic. He fervently memorialized his nation in a seventeen-volume *History of France* (1833–67) and his more famous seven-volume *History of the French Revolution* (1847–53). These populist epics celebrate France's collective march toward freedom and equality which, according to the author, culminates in the events of 1789 and 1790. France was his religion and the Revolution revealed to him the modern spirit.

Michelet's private *Journal* alerts us to the prophet's vulnerability. The diaries I have selected to translate are the spontaneous reflections of a man of genius at grips with his finitude. They include the years 1815–50, from the time his mother perished to the loss of his infant son, for Michelet remained obsessed with the sickness and death of people he loved. He modeled the *Journal* itself, his protest against bereavement, after such autobiographical masterpieces as Augustine's *Confessions,* Montaigne's *Essays,* and the *Confessions* of Jean-Jacques Rousseau. Only Michelet did not intend to publish his self-scrutinies.

At the age of twenty, he began to compose a formal autobiography, the *Memorial,* but he abandoned it for the *Journal,* to which he remained faithful until his death at age seventy-five. In public courses and more than fifty books—works of popular education as well as histories—he proclaimed an optimistic theology of history with which he justified France's destiny. His *Journal* revealed the churning anxiety at their foundation. Death, more than any other experience, guided his development as a person and as an historian.

I have entitled the selections *Mother Death* for several reasons.

First and foremost, the death of Michelet's mother when he was sixteen inaugurated his lifelong association of decay, yearning for love, guilt, and writing. She fell victim to a prolonged illness aggravated by the winter cold and malnutrition, which their poverty made it impossible to alleviate. The son had been too busy studying, that fateful night, to remain with the dying woman, and his guilt-ridden experience of her passing became the prototype of all bereavements. The demise of each loved one reawakened that fundamental loss. His first passion, little Sophie Plateau, died about five years later. When his closest male friend, Paul Poinsot, succumbed to tuberculosis at age twenty-two, Michelet discovered that writing could bring comfort.

Death was the mother of Michelet's historical vocation. Just as Montaigne had conceived his *Essays* in response to his friend Etienne de la Boétie's death, so Michelet sought to immortalize his own friendship in the *Journal*. But he had discovered this manner of inspiration much earlier. As a child, his mother would take him to the museum that housed the tombs of the French kings. Michelet's preface to his germinal book of popular education, *The People* (1846),[1] described how his artistic method grew from his empathy with figures long gone:

> My strongest childhood impression, next to reading *The Imitation of Christ*,[2] is of the Museum of French Monuments, since so shamelessly destroyed. It was there, and there only, that I received my first vivid impression of history. I would fill those tombs with my imagination and sensed the dead through the marble. And it was not without some terror that I would visit the vaults where Dagobert, Chilperic, and Fredegonda slept.

He developed feelings of intimacy with the departed. During his adolescence Michelet began to frequent the Père-Lachaise cemetery in

---

1 *The People*, trans. John P. McKay (Urbana: University of Illinois Press, 1973). Those unfamiliar with Michelet should read this very personal book and the excellent comprehensive introduction by Oscar A. Haac, *Jules Michelet* (Boston: Twayne Publishers, 1982).

2 A thirteenth-century mystical treatise presumably written by Thomas a Kempis. Michelet cherished this early influence, despite his subsequent opposition to the Church.

the east of Paris where he lived. This vast citylike necropolis, established under Napoleon, awakened the young man's panoramic conception of his nation's drama, as he strolled thoughtfully through avenues of tombstones and monuments. The cemetery was his laboratory of historical resurrection, the *Journal* its first product.

A deeper, more troubled ambition unified the *Journal*. The title *Mother Death* evokes the historian's fundamental urge to die and to be reborn. For him they seemed equivalent. As if he were on the psychoanalytic couch, he associated the lure of disease and mortality with his nostalgia for the maternal womb. He feared death, and yet he longed to surrender, to become enveloped by an all-consuming presence. He sought refuge from the contradictions of life in Mother Earth or the ocean's womb, "the Sea of Milk."[3] Powerful incestuous passions surface at crucial moments in the diaries. Michelet's need for love was so desperate that, at least in imagination, he entertained any possible return to Mother. He even conceived of a female God.

Mourning allowed him to integrate these weaknesses into a brilliant career as writer and teacher. Michelet solemnly wrote out his grief and plunged into himself through the *Journal*. A weird and sometimes magnificent poetry of bereavement arises in these pages. His marriage of love and death reminds us of our own lost loves, our sorrows; and we relive, with the author, the ancient mystery of beauty born of pain. We read with a mixture of admiration for his literary prowess and noble idealism, sorrow at the sacrifices he endured, even though we are irritated at his excessively morbid pleasures. We constantly ask: Why must it be so? Why did Michelet pursue death with such tenacity? He seemed especially to relish exhumed corpses: Poinsot; his first wife, Pauline; his father; and his infant son. With strange intensity he contemplated their remains, for such ghastly sights furthered his artistic ends. How did his literal excavation of the dead promote historical resurrection?

In the *Journal*, Michelet confronted his irreducible contradictions. With varying degrees of lucidity and courage, he attempted to resolve them and achieve inner integrity. He was a typical Romantic, ear-

[3] Michelet elaborated these fantasies in his last two nature books, *The Sea* (1861) and *The Mountain* (1868). See the Epilogue of this book, "Marriage with Mother Earth," a translation of a remarkable chapter from *The Mountain*.

nestly self-absorbed, who diligently mapped out his ideas and feelings. When his unconscious would bare itself, as it often did, he faced its testimony without embarrassment. Each stage of his life featured a personal conflict, as well as major shifts in his thinking. As a student: Could he enjoy sexual relations with women at his boardinghouse while he concentrated on his studies? Could he nurse the ailing Poinsot as he prepared for his upcoming examinations? As a professor: Need he devote more time to his wife and children, less to writing and teaching? As a widower: Was his attraction to death a problem or a precious creative method? What were the moral and religious responsibilities of the historian of France? In the *Journal*, where we expect to meet an author, we discover a man.

Jules Michelet was born in poverty on 21 August 1798 and grew up, as the later historian wrote, "like a blade of grass without sunlight between two paving stones of Paris."[4] The boy was victimized by political events. His parents were desperately poor and suffered under Napoleon's restrictions of the press, which eventually forced his father to close his print shop. Michelet, an only child, worked in his father's small establishment, even after he finally started public shcool at the age of thirteen. He was needy, shy, isolated, and brilliant. An academic career would be his salvation, and his relatives willingly sacrificed to support it.[5] He organized his days so as to harness his outstanding intellectual gifts, establishing strict habits; he rose before dawn to study or write at his oak desk and labored throughout the day. For his entire lifetime, Michelet worked relentlessly, lecturing, doing research, traveling, and producing books with amazing assiduity and dispatch.

The man was small in stature, delicate of body, armed with a powerful voice and a penetrating glance. His appearance suggested an exceptionally forceful inner life. His hair that turned white by the time he was twenty-five and his thin, tight lips betrayed the violence of his

4 From the autobiographical preface to *The People* (1846).

5 Two of his aunts donated their dowries—and consequently remained spinsters—to finance Jules's education. His grandfather, before his death, and then Uncle Narcisse, helped his father at the print shop. Later, they ran the historian's household.

contradictions. The man was lustful, ferociously egotistical, domineering, and yet generously devoted to his family, students, and democratic values. Nervous, impatient, he lived with pen in hand and soon achieved national prominence. His genius served mankind. He wrote as naturally as he breathed, and he inspired students and readers with his vast knowledge, his eloquence, and his explosive imagination.

THE TEXT AND THE TRANSLATION

Michelet's private *Journal* was a file, a deposit of experience and information, which he quoted to enliven his books and monitor his own development. This practice began in notebooks. For most of his life, however, he wrote on separate sheets of paper that he collected in folders. The methodical and frugal historian treasured every jot of his awareness, keeping the *Journal* with regularity, though sometimes neglecting it when his outside responsibilities were particularly compelling. He contributed his most abundant entries during several trips around France, England, Italy, Germany, and Switzerland—and at home in the presence of death. He always wrote quickly, sometimes in the coach in which he traveled, on the backs of envelopes, discarded manuscripts, brochures, but more often on rather large sheets. He dated his folders and scanned them systematically when he reorganized and redefined his life and ideas. Those periods usually coincided with a major loss.

The *Journal's* original French publication has a history as notorious as the biography of its author. Scholars could not consult the manuscripts until eighty-five years after Michelet's death. They fell victim, in part, when he was alive, to his second wife, Athénaïs Mialaret. She could not read the entire *Journal*, although parts she did see contained frank discussions of her husband's sexual life and his love for other women. By a sort of "retrospective jealousy" she urged Michelet to destroy many of those portions, for example, around 1853 while they vacationed in Italy. On 1 November 1864 he wrote in the *Journal* itself: "Yesterday, 31 October, my *Bible of Humanity* went on sale. I nevertheless continued to sort out my papers. Very little remains of the period that precedes my surge of 1843 against the past, my surge of 1848 toward the future." Presumably he threw out pages relating to his first wife, Pauline, who died in 1839, and to his beloved Mme Dumesnil, who died in 1842. But much remained—enough to observe how the author's love and fear of women were inseparable from his love and fear of death.

When Michelet died on 9 February 1874, everything became his widow's property. At her decease in 1899, all documents went to the historian Gabriel Monod, one of the founders of the Ecole des hautes études in Paris and a faithful disciple of Michelet. He published tantalizing selections from the *Journal* in articles about his teacher; other scholars might not consult the manuscripts. When Monod died in 1915 the intimate *Journal* was sealed and preserved at the Institut de France, of which Michelet was a member, while the rest went to the accessible Bibliothèque historique de la Ville de Paris. Not until 1951 was the diary entrusted to two candidates for the French *doctorat d'état,* Paul Viallaneix and Claude Digeon, experienced scholars charged with establishing the first integral edition. They reconstructed a text from the manuscripts dispersed at various locations and published five large volumes annotated with historical and biographical information. A delighted French public read the first two in 1959.

This is the first translation of Michelet's *Journal*. My selections are taken from his *Ecrits de jeunesse* (1818–23) and the *Journal,* volumes 1 (1828–48) and 2 (1849–60), in the editions of Paul Viallaneix. The published versions, however, do not transcribe verbatim the manuscripts, most of which were written in haste. M. Viallaneix has rectified faulty dating, completed Michelet's abbreviations, standardized his idiosyncratic punctuation, corrected misspellings, and constructed complete paragraphs where the historian had often penned lines resembling blank verse. The French editor sacrificed some of the *Journal's* spontaneous rhythm to increase its readability. My own spot checks found few substantive differences between the manuscript and the published texts, and I believe that we benefit from these primarily typographical emendations.

The selections that comprise *Mother Death* follow Michelet's first fifty-two years. My commentaries are modestly analytical; they explain biographical and historical allusions and trace the development of the historian's vocation, his changing attitudes toward the Catholic church, his struggles to find true love, and his less conscious yearnings.

My aim has been not to demonstrate a particular theory but to place the entries in their context and to help readers seize their overall coherence—as did Michelet himself when he reread the *Journal*. I have organized the chapters around the deaths of people who affected the author most intimately. The Epilogue, a chapter from *The Mountain* which I have entitled "Marriage with Mother Earth," condenses the fantasies of incest, death, and rebirth that course throughout the *Journal*. The Chronology surveys the historian's entire life and works.

The *Journal* appears here as in the French edition, except that three spaced asterisks indicate that I have omitted certain entries from a sequence. In the text itself, Michelet's own suspension points are three unspaced dots (...) that suggest thoughts or daydreams, while my ellipses are three spaced dots within square brackets ([. . .]). For specialists and nonspecialists I have added numerous explanatory notes to the ones included in the Viallaneix editions.

Michelet's prose evolved from the self-conscious formality of his adolescence to the lyrical, oratorical entries of his maturity. My translations attempt to capture, in present-day English, the flow and vitality of the original, and I hope they evoke something of the author's still compelling presence.

Chronology

1798—On 21 August Jules Michelet was born in Paris in a former convent chapel. His father, Jean-François-Furcy Michelet (born December 1769), a native of Laon, ran a small print shop. His mother, Angélique-Constance Millet, was born in 1761 of a peasant family in Renwez, the Ardennes.

1800—The Michelet family moved to the rue Montmartre, then the rue du Jour (1801), then the rue Française (1802).

1808—They moved to the rue des Saints-Pères and Michelet's father was imprisoned for debts at Sainte-Pélagie. He was freed the following year and the family moved to the boulevard Saint-Martin.

1809—Michelet learned to set type in his father's print shop and began his studies in 1810 with a grammarian and former Jacobin named Mélot, who also tutored Paul Poinsot. In 1811, the Michelets moved to the rue Notre-Dame-de-Nazareth.

1812—An official Napoleonic decree of February 1810 limited the number of Parisian printers to sixty; Michelet's father lost his livelihood. In October Jules entered the Collège Charlemagne after private tutoring. In 1813 another move.

1815—On 9 February Michelet's mother died at their apartment on the rue de Périgueux where they had moved in January 1814. In October 1815, he and his father then moved to Dr. Duchemin's nursing home (rue de Buffon) at which he was administrator with Mme Fourcy and Jules entered the *Rhétorique* class (the final year) at the Collège Charlemagne. Mme Fourcy became a "second mother" to him.

1817–19—Michelet earned his degrees: *baccalauréat, license, doctorat ès lettres* (theses on Plutarch and on Locke). In 1816 he obtained the first prizes in French oratory and in Latin translation in the *Concours général*. He now made his living as an instructor at the Briand Institute. In July 1818 Pauline Rousseau became his mistress. They all moved to no. 49, rue de la Roquette, which his father ran as a boardinghouse. From 1818 on he kept a regular, almost daily private diary in which he noted his readings, projects for teaching and writing, travels, intimate thoughts, etc.

1821–23 — His closest friend, Paul Poinsot, died on 14 February 1821. Michelet won third place in the newly established national examination, the *agrégation des lettres,* in September. He was appointed professor at the Collège Charlemagne; and in 1822 at the Collège Sainte-Barbe. Mme Fourcy died in December 1823.

1824 — On 20 May Michelet married the pregnant Pauline Rousseau in a religious ceremony. He was to have two children with her: Adèle (born 28 August 1824) and Charles (born 17 November 1829). Encouraged by Victor Cousin, he undertook the translation of Vico's *Scienza nuova.*

1825 — At the home of Victor Cousin, Michelet met Edgar Quinet (translator of Herder) and began a lifelong friendship. In June Michelet published his first book, a school manual, *Chronological Tableau of Modern History* (1453–1789).

1827 — Michelet was appointed professor of history and philosophy at the Ecole normale. In March he published his translation of Vico's *Principles of Philosophy and History*. In April he moved to no. 27, rue de l'Arbalète.

1828 — He traveled in Germany from August to September. Upon his return to Paris he became tutor to the nine-year-old granddaughter of Charles X of France.

1829 — He gave up his philosophy course at the Ecole normale. In November he devoted his teaching to Roman history.

1830 — During the spring Michelet traveled in Italy. Following the July Revolution he was chosen as tutor to the thirteen-year-old Princess Clémentine, fifth child of Louis-Philippe. In October he was named head of the historical section of the Archives.

1831 — In April his *Introduction to Universal History* was published, and in July his *History of the Roman Republic*. The family moved to the rue des Fossés-Saint-Victor.

1833—On 21 November Michelet began to substitute for François Guizot at the Sorbonne in the chair of modern history. Volumes 1 and 2 of the *History of France* (up to 1270) were published on 21 December. Thus began his life's "monument."

1834–36—From 5 August to 5 September he made a trip to England during which he discovered the industrial world. In 1836 the family moved to no. 12, rue des Postes, where Michelet remained until his second marriage in 1849.

1837—Volume 3 of the *History of France* (1270–1380) appeared in June, as did *The Origins of French Law*. He traveled in Belgium and Holland, 22 June to 18 July.

1838—Michelet was elected to the chair of "history and moral philosophy" at the Collège de France on 13 February. In March he was elected to the Académie des sciences morales et politiques. He witnessed Poinsot's exhumation on 25 April. He taught his first course at the Collège de France from 23 April to July. He traveled to Belgium and Northern Italy from 8 July to 17 August.

1839—From 24 March to 7 April Michelet traveled to Lyon, where he researched the conditions of the working classes. On 24 July Pauline died from tuberculosis aggravated by alcoholism. Michelet experienced great remorse at having sacrificed his wife to his constant work. He had her corpse exhumed and moved to another grave in September.

1840—Volume 4 of the *History of France* (1380–1422) appeared in February. Around this time he began an ardent but chaste friendship with Mme Adèle Dumesnil, whose son Alfred was an enthusiastic student of his at the Collège de France.

1841—Mme Dumesnil, suffering from cancer of the reproductive organs, moved into Michelet's apartment, rue des Postes. On 23 August volume 5 of the *History of France* (Joan of Arc) was published, showing evidence of his feelings for Mme Dumesnil.

1842—On 31 May Mme Dumesnil died after an agonizing illness. Accompanied by his children and by Alfred Dumesnil, Michelet traveled in Germany (19 June–30 July) in an effort to dispel his grief. During this period he sought support in natural science for his belief in personal immortality.

1843–44—In July Michelet published courses he gave with Edgar Quinet at the Collège de France, entitled *The Jesuits.* On 3 August, Alfred Dumesnil, the son of Michelet's deceased friend, married Adèle Michelet. Michelet then traveled to Switzerland with Charles. Volume 6 of the *History of France* was published in January 1844.

1845—*About Priests, Women, and the Family* was published on 15 January and put on the Index in April. There were violent clerical attacks against the teachings of Michelet and Edgar Quinet.

1846—*The People,* the summa of Michelet's utopian program, was published on 28 January. His father died at seventy-six years of age on 18 November. Michelet had interrupted his monumental *History of France* to undertake the *History of the French Revolution,* for which he is now best known.

1847—Volumes 1 and 2 of the *French Revolution* appeared in February and in November. Michelet traveled to Holland and wrote a letter to Frederick-William, king of Prussia, soliciting money for Polish insurgents.

1848—On 2 January the Guizot government suspended Michelet's course at the Collège de France. In February the revolution broke out. In March Michelet and Quinet solemnly resumed their lectures. Michelet was recognized as one of the spiritual leaders of the restored Republic. In November he met and fell in love with Athénaïs Mialaret, an orphan (born 1826) who worked as a governess for the Cantacuzène family, then living in Vienna.

1849—Volume 3 of the *History of the French Revolution* was published on 10 February. On 12 March he married Athénaïs in a civil ceremony. In his course at the Collège de France, he extolled the cause of love and of popular education.

1850—On 10 February volume 4 of the *French Revolution* appeared. On 2 July Athénaïs gave birth to their only child, Yves-Jean-Lazare, who died on 24 August. Michelet had his father's corpse exhumed on 31 August and reburied with the infant on 11 September.

1851—Michelet's course was suspended on 13 March because of noisy demonstrations by his students against Louis-Napoleon; there were many protests against this measure. In the spring volume 5 of the

French Revolution was published. On 24 October Michelet refused the retirement at half-salary that the government offered him. Part of *The Golden Legend* under the title *Poland and Russia: The Legend of Kosciusko* appeared in November.

1852—Michelet refused the oath of allegiance to the Second Empire and was officially removed from the Collège de France and the Archives. In June he withdrew in semiexile to Nantes.

1853—Michelet fell ill in March. On 1 August volumes 6 and 7 of the *History of the French Revolution* appeared. Exhausted and depressed, he spent the winter at Nervi, Italy, near Genoa, recovering slowly.

1854—*Democratic Legends of the North* appeared on 21 January. *Women of the French Revolution* was published the same month. Michelet sojourned at Genoa, Turin, and Acqui (5–30 June), where he took remarkable therapeutic mud baths and formulated a philosophy of nature. He then returned to Paris.

1855—He published volume 7 of his *History of France* (*The Renaissance*) on 1 February. He began *The Bird* from 21 April to 2 July under the influence of Athénaïs. On 2 July volume 8 of the *History of France* (*The Reformation*) appeared. He traveled to Belgium and Holland. On 15 July his daughter, Adèle Dumesnil, died of tuberculosis. Michelet returned to Paris for the funeral.

1856—Volume 9 of the *History of France* (*The Wars of Religion*) appeared on 8 March. *The Bird*, Michelet's first nature book, was published on 12 March. From July to September Michelet traveled in Switzerland. On 10 November volume 10 of the *History of France* (*The League of Henri IV*) was put on sale.

1857—Volume 11 of the *History of France* (*Henry IV and Richelieu*) appeared on 27 May. The Michelets spent the summer in Fontainebleau, where he wrote *The Insect*, published in October. In December the couple left for Hyères, where they remained for several months.

1858—Volume 12 of the *History of France* (*Richelieu and the Fronde*) appeared in March. Summer visits were made to Granville and Pornic in Brittany. On 17 November Michelet published *Love*, followed by *Woman* in November 1859.

1860—Volume 13 of the *History of France* (*Louis XIV and the Revocation of the Edict of Nantes*) was published in April. Michelet visited Rouen, Vascoeuil, and Etretat, where he finished *The Sea*, begun in April; it was published on 15 January 1861.

1862—Volume 14 of the *History of France* (*Louis XIV and the Duke of Burgundy*) appeared in February. Michelet's son Charles died of tuberculosis on 16 April. On 7 November the publisher Hachette refused to sell *The Witch*, fearing a scandal and a seizure. The work was published by Dentu and Hetzel.

1863—Volume 15 of the *History of France* (*The Regency*) went on sale in October.

1864—After a summer sojourn in Normandy, Michelet published *The Bible of Humanity* on 31 October. In November Michelet began an extensive reexamination of his past; he sorted notes from his private diary and, encouraged by his wife, burned many of them.

1867—The Michelets sojourned in Veytaux and in Switzerland. The final volume of the *History of France* (*Louis XVI*), volume 17, appeared on 10 October, volume 16 (*Louis XV*) having been published in May 1866. *The Witch* and *The Bird* (in a new, illustrated edition) were reissued. On 1 February 1868 *The Mountain* was published.

1869—In January Michelet's *History of the French Revolution* was republished with a new preface. In September he completed a long and important autobiographical preface to the Lacroix edition of the *History of France*. On 12 November *Our Sons* appeared.

1870—Michelet began work on his *History of the Nineteenth Century*. On 5 August, following the declaration of war on Prussia, Michelet signed the peace manifesto drawn up in London by Marx, Engels, and Louis Blanc. Michelet was at Montreux when the Second Empire fell. On 29 October he went to Florence, where he remained for a while.

1871—Michelet wrote *France before the Eyes of Europe* with the hope of ending his country's moral isolation; it appeared on 25 January. He had his first stroke on 30 April. On 22 May, upon learning of the collapse of the Commune, he was stricken a second time. He temporarily lost his speech and the use of his right hand. He left for Switzerland on 20 June and returned to Hyères in October.

1872—Volume 1 of the *History of the Nineteenth Century* was published on 3 April. Michelet returned to Paris in May. In October his chest became inflamed and his right hand partly paralyzed.

1873—Volume 2 of the *History of the Nineteenth Century* appeared on 15 March. In the summer the Michelets vacationed in Switzerland, in the Alps, then at Hyères, where he finished volume 3 of his *History of the Nineteenth Century.*

1874—In January he drafted a preface for volume 3: the book was ready. On 9 February he died of a heart attack.

Prologue
A Memorial to Mother and Friend

JEAN-FELIX MICHELET
November 1747–September 1814

ANGÉLIQUE-CONSTANCE MILLET MICHELET
1761–9 February 1815

PAUL BENOIST POINSOT
2 June 1798–14 February 1821

– Dead! That seemed incomprehensible to me. It is strange that I am unable to fear the death of those who are very dear to me, nor can I conceive of it when it occurs. I think that those I love are immortal. *Memorial* (1822) –

– THE YOUTHFUL *Memorial* provides a lucid prologue to the *Journal* that Michelet continued for his entire life. He conceived both records in order to preserve his intimacy with Paul Poinsot and to relieve the emptiness caused by his absence. Michelet inaugurated a *Journal* on 4 May 1820, the very day his closest friend left Paris for residency at the hospital in Bicêtre, just outside the city limits. At Poinsot's departure, Michelet began systematically to commune with himself. Exactly one month later, on 4 June 1820, he deliberately marked the anniversary by undertaking an autobiography called the *Memorial.* Michelet hoped to consolidate the insights scattered in the *Journal,* to plan future actions by analyzing the past, and to leave a permanent imprint should he die young. He proudly proclaimed, in the first paragraph, that the *Memorial* would measure up to Rousseau's *Confessions.*[1]

The *Memorial* began by describing his family's financial want and the print shop in which he set type with his father. The boy alluded to his licentious conversations with workers around the time of his mother's final decline. He acknowledged that she had often blamed her husband for the family's misfortunes. The son's account barely concealed his anger at her sickness, her bad moods, and the abandonment caused by her eventual death while he blamed himself, indirectly, for siding with his father in his parents' quarrels. And yet, deploring his own "violent character," the boy recalled that, at age four, he maliciously hit his father on the head with a stick.

Michelet had completed over eighty-four notebook pages of this confession by November 1820; they detailed his conflict-ridden home life, readings, thoughts, and reflections on female infatuations and male friendships. Then for about sixteen months he neglected the *Memorial.* He was absorbed in preparations for the *agrégation,* the national examination that would guarantee him a job in the university system. His ambition coincided with the misfortune of his dearest friend's fatal illness. Poinsot contracted tuberculosis and perished on

1 The *Confessions* of Jean-Jacques Rousseau (1712–78) were published posthumously in 1781 and 1788.

14 February 1821. Michelet returned to the *Memorial* over a year later, on 31 March 1822. It remained unfinished.

The death of Michelet's mother figured eminently in the *Memorial*. I have translated the final section, written in 1822, which reveals how her death aroused her son's religious perplexities, sexual desires, and probably conditioned his lifelong responses to loss. Michelet wrote the pages published below (numbers 89–97 of the ninety-eight-page manuscript) under the shadow of Poinsot's recent demise when the friends were twenty-two. The narrator recalled Poinsot's return to Paris from boarding school in 1814, when they were fifteen. He then associated that mortal event with the deaths of his grandfather and mother.

[. . .] My dear Poinsot's return more effectively made me forget the sorrow of my household. He had come back from Melun and was restored to me forever. He had studied at the Pharmacy School for a few years and was to establish himself in Paris after that. Nothing could separate us anymore... My dear friend, how did it happen that you died before me? How could such a union be broken? *Siccine dividit amara mors.* [Thus bitter death divides.][2] I shall never recall without sadness our long walks, which we could never get ourselves to end. So many times we would accompany each other home, two or three times, back and forth! My God, how right we were to prolong the time we spent together.

At that time my soul was hardly calmer than it is now, for it seems that I am destined never to rest. He listened patiently to everything, too much perhaps for his own peace of mind, for passions are contagious. But friendship was so strong in his pure soul that it silenced all passions; everything resolved itself in the face of that powerful feeling. He said to me: "If you enlist" (for war was then widely discussed), "I don't want to enlist as a pharmacist. I will follow you as a

2 Michelet first wrote this Latin quotation from Horace in the *Journal* entry of 6 July 1821, a few months after Poinsot's death. He used it again in his wife's epitaph in 1839 (see chap. 2).

soldier." Those words sank into my heart; they pierce it now. See what I have lost!

Since that time I endured the great loss of my granddad who loved me so and who had fruitlessly taken such trouble to teach me music.[3] A long neglected injury became a sort of ulcer, and it was too late to operate on him. I still see the bench upon which I found him seated at the place Royale,[4] when he had just received his terrible condemnation from the surgeon's lips. The disease constantly worsened; gangrene developed in the hot summer days and soon carried him off. It is horrible to say, but, a week before his death, maggots were already active in his wound. I must not omit one very simple remark which, however, moved me deeply. It was shortly after the event, there was a great storm; my grandmother began to cry and said: "It is raining on him." I was perhaps more deeply moved than at his death itself.

A little while later, I entered my next-to-last year, and *collège* became even less disagreeable. The instructor's civility and ease removed what remained of the school's grimness and harshness.[5] In exchange, my home became even sadder. Mother became sicker and sicker. Hydropsy, which often terminates such illnesses, had declared itself a long time ago, and my heart filled with sinister forebodings. However, the deplorable violence of my character was such that sometimes harsh words escaped me, for which I now wish with all my blood to atone, especially those I spoke when I had just given the school fifty francs which we so badly needed. I had barely pronounced those cruel words when I felt ripped apart, but some unknown evil shame kept me from begging pardon while there was still time.

In the meantime, the hydropsy spread from her legs to her body and Mother could no longer move. One rather cold evening I went out for

3 Félix Michelet had been concertmaster of the Cathedral of Laon, his hometown, until the Revolution of 1789.

4 At present the place des Vosges near the Bastille in Paris.

5 Inspired by the elderly teacher M. Carré, Michelet became the most outstanding pupil of his class in 1814–15 at the Collège Charlemagne.

a moment to take a walk on the boulevard. When I returned, I could see flames coming out of a neighboring chimney and falling into a courtyard where there were casks of alcohol... Imagine, Mother could not be moved! It is the most horrible anguish I have experienced in my life. Fortunately, the fire soon went out.

Mother needed continual care because she could not move; and I remember only with veneration and gratitude Papa's behavior in those sad circumstances. But he had to be away part of the day. They didn't want to interrupt my studies, so we had to hire a caretaker, despite our bitter poverty. My grandmother sent us a woman, one of her neighbors (named Leroy), to be at our house only during the day; during the night, Papa would constantly get up.

Mother was not unaware of her condition. In fact, she was rather surprised at having been able to suffer for so long, and fearlessly she anticipated the end of a life of sorrow and deprivation. She sometimes spoke of her approaching death with a strange indifference. One day, as her bed sheets were being made, she said: "Put that one aside for my shroud." Sometime later she contracted sores from remaining in bed. She told us she would die as soon as the sores dried, that she had always heard it happened like that.

On Ash Wednesday (8 February 1815), the day before our return to class after the Shrovetide vacation, I had gone to the passage des Jacobins to buy some books and see M. Mélot, who lived there at the time. The weather was very cloudy and very gloomy. When I returned I found Mother sicker. She had difficulty breathing and constantly asked for someone to prop her up on her pillows; the swelling seemed to smother her. I spent part of the night doing next day's homework, and I have preserved it as a monument to that unhappy night.[6] I continually had to prop her up. Toward midnight she told me to go to sleep and, if my memory is accurate, she seemed touched by my care.

In the morning, when I awoke, I saw Papa weeping, and he told me:

---

6 The boy was translating a Latin text by Seneca on the fear of death.

"Your mother is dead."

Dead! That seemed incomprehensible to me. It is strange that I am unable to fear the death of those who are very dear to me, nor can I conceive of it when it occurs. I think that those I love are immortal.

I spent the day with my eyes fixed on Mama and reading from time to time the prayers for the dead at the same table where I now write. Death had not changed her at all. Such a long illness had so altered her appearance that one might have thought her dead a long time before. Her face had somewhat sunken without becoming horrifying. Her lower lip protruded a little over the other, almost as in her sleep when she seemed to breathe while dozing.

My most violent outburst of grief occurred when we returned from the funeral procession. Her brother Millet, who was there with us, came to our home to have something to drink. That large, bare bedroom, that solitude wrenched my soul. During the entire month while we still lived in that apartment, I walked only on tiptoe and I was always afraid to make noise. I experienced a new grief when I came to my senses and realized how futile those precautions were.

However, I was less moved by that cruel event at that time than I would have been at any other. The change of life and location that soon followed prevented the blow from sinking in so deeply.[7] A freedom I had not known until then, a gentler and less anxious existence, were powerful consolations for a sixteen-year-old child. Sometimes I was astonished, I was ashamed of my hardness of heart. My cruel happiness made me feel guilty, as if I had acquired it at the price of her life. But outside, a multitude of distractions, and within me, a multitude of passions nourished in solitude, and which surged forth hoping to be satisfied, made it quite difficult to return to the past. I was living altogether in the future.

7 They moved from the dreary basement apartment on the rue de Périgueux to a boardinghouse at no. 7, rue de Buffon, near the Jardin des Plantes. There the young man enjoyed the botanical gardens and natural history museum.

All my work habits and assiduous studies were completely disrupted. When he returned from work at M. Duchemin's boardinghouse, and after our frugal meal, Papa would take me out and we went for long walks. The first one was to the Tuileries, on a warm and overcast spring day. I remember it very distinctly. On that first day of freedom, it seemed as if I saw the world opening before me, "*waste and wide*" as Romeo said.[8]

Sometimes, in the evenings, we would also go to my aunt's house. And among other people who gathered in her shop, I noticed a Mme Moisant, a very pretty little woman but of poor breeding. I later learned that you could easily spend an hour at her house for twenty francs a head.

Sometimes we also visited the recently widowed Mme Renneville and her daughter, who chattered rather well and who drew quite prettily. Together we discussed love affairs, but I was so timid!

Someone I liked much more was little Sophie Plateau,[9] for whom I had already begun to entertain very tender feelings a long time before. We would sometimes take her family for a walk, and since they remained behind us, I had whole hours of private conversation. But those hours advanced my affair but little. Most women are moved, not by the endearments of an honest heart, but by praise. We must make them laugh, entertain them, talk about their beauty; and no one knew how to do that worse than I. I enjoyed the sweet pleasure of being alone, as it were, with a pretty little person who was nice and upright, also her mother's support, and her brother's example. I was happy to be with her, even when we talked about the most unimportant things. The impossibility of getting any more (since we saw each other only on those walks) subdued my desires; and, when I walked arm in arm with her, I could not imagine a sweeter situation. Only occasionally, a

8 Michelet quotes Shakespeare in English.

9 Sophie Plateau was about twelve years old when she and Jules first met. She died during her adolescence. Michelet first notes his search for her grave on 13 September 1820.

very keen feeling of happiness made me gently squeeze her arm or take her hand to see if the mist had chilled it too much. The girl allowed me to do this, but it must have been quite confusing for her to reconcile those liberties with the apparent coolness of my conversation.

I toyed with the idea of not confining myself to these innocent familiarities. Twice I even went to her house rather inflamed with passion. But there always remained a rampart of courtesy between us that was impossible to breach. Except for those two visits, I hardly saw her as anything more than my sister. A woman without vivacity, as pretty as she may be, never inspires very violent desires.

That is how we spent the evenings. [. . .]

MICHELET'S MOURNING PROCESS

–These closing pages of the *Memorial* show Michelet's utter preoccupation with his mournful emotions. Guilt guided his thoughts about Poinsot's premature death: "My dear friend, how did it happen that you died before me?" he lamented, denying his relief at not being in the grave. Michelet tried to repent by splitting the partnership into good and evil: the deceased retained his "pure soul" while the lonely survivor faced his unruly passions. The *Memorial* itself was an act of reparation. Michelet wrote an idealized story of their friendship in order to immortalize a purified past. The history of Poinsot was already a fictional resurrection.

Death was truly the mother of his most intense feelings. His fascination began around 1815, when his mother died. From the first, bereaved women stimulated his imagination. After his grandfather perished the year before, the boy noticed that his grandmother's sorrow—intensified in his fantasy by the violent storm—had aroused his pain more than the old man's demise itself. Her simple expression of mournful love unblocked his feelings.

His mother's death provoked complex responses because his love for her mixed bitterness with affection. On their final evening he was busy with homework; and when she passed he was asleep, absent. As if to sidestep her posthumous judgment, he timidly wrote: "if my memory is accurate, she seemed touched by my care." He preserved his assignment "as a monument to that unhappy night." All his writings became a memorial to such neglect.

His mourning progressed by stages. He first denied her death outright: "It is strange that I am unable to fear the death of those who are very dear to me, nor can I conceive of it when it occurs." To verify the fact he examined his mother's corpse, admiring her spirit while contemplating her gross remains. As a mature thinker he would challenge decay with ingenious theories of immortality. Following his initial denial, the young man struggled with contradictory feelings: his poignant sense of loss and his real (and acknowledged) joy at becoming liberated. He minimized his mother's ill temper, which the opening pages of the *Memorial*, written before Poinsot's death, readily admit. He extolled her resignation while cursing his "violent character" and stubborn pride. Mother appeared glorified and the son evil. Denial then returned. During the deathwatch he stared at her corpse, read funeral prayers, but could not let her go: "Her lower lip protruded a little over the other, almost as in her sleep." True mourning was delayed until he returned from the cemetery: "That large, bare bedroom, that solitude wrenched my soul." Still, for the following month, Michelet acted as if she were alive and bothered by noise; he walked on tiptoe until he finally "came to [his] senses" and "experienced a new grief." Though he was no longer angered by his mother's illness, he remained guilt-ridden: "My cruel happiness made me feel [. . .] as if I had acquired it at the price of her life."

But father and son truly enjoyed their "cruel happiness." The sixteen-year-old and forty-five-year-old men zestfully sought female companionship, visiting young widows who had attractive daughters. The adolescent's lust remained purely imaginary, however, until they moved into the boardinghouse at no. 7, rue de Buffon, near the Jardin des Plantes, where his father had found work the previous year. The boy did not realize, as he wrote the last pages of the *Memorial* in 1822, how much he savored older women.

Readers of Michelet's *Journal* are bewildered by his devotion to death. Why does he study his pain with such ardor? And why does he also, paradoxically, refuse to accept his loved ones' departures? The *Memorial*, composed seven years after his mother's death, opens the mysteries of the *Journal*, written in the presence of corpses.

1 The Death of My Dearest Friend

SOPHIE PLATEAU
c. 1797–c. 1820

PAUL BENOIST POINSOT
2 June 1798–14 February 1821

ANNE-MADELEINE CHRISTOPHE FOURCY
c. 1767–December 1823

– Oh! Why did I not take more advantage of the time when I could see you? I should have embraced you without respite until death froze you in my arms.
Journal, 14 February 1821 –

– FRIENDSHIP AMONG men has always been a bond as sacred as family. This was especially true for the passionate but isolated Jules Michelet, who craved companionship for his dreams and thoughts. When he was eleven years old he found his perfect confidant in Paul Poinsot. They first met in 1810 at the house of their Latin tutor, M. Mélot. Michelet's parents had just sent him to this former Jacobin to begin his education. Not until two years later, at the age of thirteen, did he enter a public school, the Collège Charlemagne. By the time he earned the *baccalauréat* in 1817, Poinsot had become a spiritual brother. They separated to pursue different callings. Paul was preparing to become first a pharmacist, later a physician, while Jules, who had won national competitions in Latin and French, was destined for a career of scholarship.

Michelet also needed to love a woman. Soon after his mother's death in February 1815, he and his father moved into Dr. Duchemin's sanitorium for the physically and mentally infirm. The adolescent found another mother in Mme Fourcy, the woman who had given his father the job, a forty-eight-year-old widow who managed the establishment. She had three children of her own and welcomed the boy into her brood. In 1816, when one of her daughters, Marianne, killed herself after being abandoned by her lover, the adoptive son's feelings for his *bonne maman* (as he called her) blossomed into an ambiguous passion. Moved by her bereavement, Michelet composed a fervently lyrical poem meant to console her sorrow.[1] They began to have sexual relations.

Michelet's liaison reminds us of Jean-Jacques Rousseau and his first mistress, Mme de Warens. In his *Confessions* Rousseau describes how this generous woman, twelve years his senior, became his religious advisor (by converting him to Catholicism), his lover, and a substitute mother. He even called her *Maman!* Michelet, for his part, had always been sensitive to older suffering women. But his amorous involvement with Mme Fourcy after her daughter's suicide did not compromise her maternal authority; she was a devout Catholic who fostered

1 The poem began: "Heart too sensitive, too strict virtue / Graciousness, talent, mildness, beauty / Death has devoured all: / Take pity on a mother's sorrow."

Michelet's religious aspirations. Despite his father's anticlericalism, he was baptized on 23 June 1816, with Mme Fourcy as godmother and Poinsot as godfather.

At the beginning of 1817, Michelet found a more appropriate object for his desire. He met the twenty-five-year-old Pauline Rousseau, a plump, not very pretty, but lusty and compliant young woman—only six years his elder—who lived at the home as the paid companion of the old and demented marquise de Rouhault. They soon established a quasi-conjugal relationship. When Poinsot came to live with them that year, the new "family" was virtually complete. In July 1818, after Dr. Duchemin closed the home, godmother, father, son, his mistress, and his pal all moved to no. 49, rue de la Roquette.

Michelet's studies benefited from this arrangement, which would later cause him moral anguish. He received the *baccalauréat* in May 1817 and passed his *license ès lettres* in July 1818, the same month they moved. He then set to work on his *doctorat ès lettres* which, at the time, required only two short memoirs, one in French, one in Latin. He defended theses on Plutarch and Locke in 1819 and had thus launched his academic career.

Poinsot left the household at rue de la Roquette on 4 May 1820 to pursue advanced medical studies at the Bicêtre hospital. But he soon fell ill with tuberculosis. Michelet followed his friend's demise with rapt attention, recording in the *Journal* the subtle modalities of his anxiety about Poinsot and guilt at his steadfast ambition. Our selections start on the day Poinsot died, 14 February 1821. The survivor wrote directly to the corpse during the lonely night vigil beside it.

14 February 1821, Wednesday

Two steps from your body which no longer hears me, I continue this *Journal* which I had begun for you. It is impossible for me to surrender all hope. God is just; a just man need not die altogether. Surely we will see each other again.

How can it be that two souls, which had never engaged in thought apart from one another, are so cruelly separated? How can I now make your soul hear mine? Meanwhile, your soul exists, for God is just. Hear me, then, wherever you may be.

Yes, my dear friend, I will speak with you forever. Without a doubt, freed of your physical senses, you understand me all the better.

What terrifies me about death is that we leave those we love only to see them fall into the hands of an all-powerful Being who, because He is Himself perfect, must judge virtue all the more severely. But, dear friend, I fear nothing for you. How could so pure a life have offended God? How many good intentions could you not place before Him! Will that sublime love of virtue with which I so often saw you imbued not counterbalance the slight weakness that one could blame in your life?

Oh, my dear friend, do you still remember that day when, seated together behind a haystack in the Gentilly meadow, we discussed the immortality of the soul? What more worthy offering than those pure conversations? And the day when we sat in the Glacière meadow? Oh, my friend, you probably hear me, but you no longer answer:

> *...Tene, vita frater amabilior*
> *Aspiciam numquam, at certe semper amabo!*
> [And you, brother more beloved than life,
> I will never see you again, but I will
> certainly love you forever!][2]

Oh! Why did I not take more advantage of the time when I could see you? I should have embraced you without respite until death froze you in my arms.

Unhappy child, your eyes sought me at your last moment of life. You might have believed for an instant that Jules neglected you. Oh! I was the one who should have closed your eyes! Woe to me! I deserve to have no one to close mine.[3]

---

2 Michelet paraphrases these lines, quoted in Montaigne's essay *Of Friendship, Essays*, book 1, chap. 28, in which the author mourns the death of Etienne de la Boétie. Montaigne cites Catullus (book 4, lines 10–11), who exclaimed before his brother died: "*Numquam ego te, vita frater amabilior, / Aspiciam posthac; at certe semper amabo*."

3 At the news of Poinsot's agony, Michelet rushed to his home but arrived too late to hear his final words.

And how can I ever repent those cruel words that impatience made me utter several days before? Now you are aware of them, perhaps you will forgive me. But my cruel words remain forever on my conscience.

But I truly loved you, as harsh and impatient as I might have been. Once, on a similar day, when you lived on the rue des Anglais, you walked with me until we reached the Pont Marie and, the minute I left you, my eyes filled with tears. I was already at the Port Saint-Paul when I saw that you stayed on the bridge as we continued to look at each other.[4] Poor friend, a bad diet was already undermining your health, and I had a sad foreboding of some unknown misfortune.

21 February 1821, Wednesday
(Eight days after Poinsot's death)
I at first hesitated whether to write about what happened during that sad week, whose events are so deeply engraved in my mind: *Quanquam animus meminisse horret...* [Although these memories constrict my heart with horror].[5]

No matter. It would be selfish, cowardly, to avoid examining them.

Monday, I went with Pauline to Poinsot's house, and I was deeply moved by the change in his appearance and complexion. I had to go near the fireplace to hide my tears. Then Pauline arrived and felt the same emotion. I was afraid that he would see her cry, and I made an effort to keep my eyes dry and calm my expression. Seated at the foot of his bed, I was holding the *Memoirs* of Tott,[6] but I kept looking at him. While he, each time he opened his eyes, he fixed them on me. He had tremendous difficulty breathing, and he could hear only with great effort. At the moment we left, his mother gave him a purse.

---

4 The rue des Anglais, which still exists, is near place Maubert. The Port Saint-Paul, known now as the Quai des Célestins, is near the rue Saint-Paul that Michelet took to reach the rue Saint-Antoine, in the direction of place de la Bastille and rue de la Roquette. One can walk those streets today.

5 Virgil, *The Aeneid*, book 2, line 12.

6 François, baron de Tott (1733–93), a diplomat under Louis XV and Louis XVI, published *Mémoires sur les Turcs et les Tartares* (1784).

Thanking her, he said that he would use it as soon as he could go out again.

The next day (on Tuesday, the last day I saw him), in a very cold and very black fog, I went to Mme Villemain's house[7] and, from there, to Poinsot. I found that he could hear, and I thought he was better. The nurse did not agree; and, in fact, his breathing difficulty had not abated. We waited for M. Surville.[8] I went to his home, but in vain. Upon my return, I saw Poinsot again for a short while and, about five o'clock, I bid him good-bye. He gave me his hand with some energy, contrary to custom, and tenderly shook mine. It was the last time. As I left, I said to his sister: "Do you think something will happen before tomorrow?" "No," she said. I left, unable to say a single word to her. My heart was bursting.

Wednesday, the fourteenth, quite unfortunately, was the anniversary of the duc de Berry's assassination.[9] Contrary to my usual practice, I tutored Roussel from eight to nine. During that time, they looked everywhere for me. It was only as I was quite absentmindedly leaving the Briand Institute that the doorkeeper said to me: "One of your friends is dying." The fog seemed to thicken around me; I cannot express how everything suddenly changed. I began to run without stopping. It was too late. I found Virginie in tears: "Oh! My God!" I flung myself into the bedroom. There was no longer a friend there; I saw only a still-warm body which seemed to sleep. "Oh! Monsieur,

---

7 Michelet seeks the emotional support of his former teacher, the literary historian, Abel-François Villemain (1790–1870). Villemain began his brilliant career in 1810 at the Collège Charlemagne, where he inspired and singled out the young Michelet. He taught literature at the Ecole normale from 1811 on as well, and from 1815 at the Sorbonne. Villemain faithfully promoted Michelet's career: in 1821 he encouraged him to take the *agrégation* examination; in 1827 he helped him get a post at the Ecole normale; in 1843, after Villemain had become minister of education, he defended Michelet's courses against the Jesuits at the Collège de France.

8 The physician.

9 Charles, duc de Berry (born 1778), the second son of Charles X, was killed by Louvel on 13 February 1820, as he was leaving the opera. He was a favorite of the ultra-Royalists during the Restoration.

he died calling your name." I was collapsing. I took his hand, still warm and not yet stiff, and I kissed it. But where was his soul, so pure and so tender? "Dear child, dear child!" That was the only name I could call him. And, in fact, during the last years, I cared for him with a father's heart.

I asked his brother if they would give him a tomb and I offered to contribute if they needed money; he seemed irritated by my indiscretion.[10] Then Mme Fourcy and Pauline arrived. Then Papa. I accompanied them to the faubourg du Temple to the home of one of Mme Poinsot's sisters, where his mother was. We found her plunged in tears. And her pain made my own tears flow with renewed abundance. When I entered, she embraced me with an outburst of feeling: "Oh, dear friend of my son, you will be mine." Three children, including one of Poinsot's sisters, were crying as much as we. Several times, I was ready to rush forward to grasp these poor children in my arms. I could not help taking hold of his little sister. "Oh!" I said to the mother, "I will be so attached to these children!" I accompanied the ladies to the rue des Trois-Bornes, which I then walked down to deliver some messages to Virginie. In the evening, I prepared myself to spend the night beside the body; and I felt so ill at ease that I wanted Papa to accompany me. He was kind enough to do so.

During that cruel night, my thoughts flowed with extreme slowness. My body was so overwhelmed that my mind tormented me less. I brought a pen and some ink into the room, and I tried to overcome the stupor that absorbed me by writing to my poor friend, whose body was beside me. A crucifix and some holy water were placed upon him, and a candle burned in front of the closed curtains. This gloomy display permeated my suffering with a nameless dread. His father came and wanted to take our place. We remained, as was proper. Before going to

10 In nineteenth-century France, as today, a family could choose either a temporary or a permanent gravesite. See below, entry of 25 April 1838, for Poinsot's exhumation.

bed, he lifted the shroud and we looked at this poor friend. He was radiantly beautiful. His skin, whiter than it had ever been, and his black hair created a contrast which, were it not for the calm and angelic gentleness of the face, would have had something frightful about it. But the skin was cold and hard. To the touch, it was already of the earth; it made me shiver with horror and pain. That body, so well-tended just a short time ago, passed such a cold night on straw! At six o'clock, I looked at him again and said aloud: "Farewell." That was, I believe, the moment of most stabbing pain.

I went out then, giving my arm to Papa. The night was ghastly and lined with an icy fog. I thought my tears were freezing on my cheeks. I was put to bed when I returned home, and I was up at eleven o'clock. Poret[11] came soon after. He had just received the message; I was extremely touched by his zeal.

When we arrived, the coffin was in the doorway and many people had already assembled. Alas! What indifference they showed! It wrung my heart. Among all those people, I alone had been intimate with him. I had to ask Poret to hold a corner of the shroud. The moment we entered the church, I noticed that I was not the only one crying. His brothers, they were not crying. At that moment, I felt that Poret would become Poinsot's heir. I was upset in that church in many different ways. But after a gloomy hymn, at the moment the cross was suddenly raised, I felt my tears dry up briefly. My thoughts of God and immortality awakened. When we arrived at the cemetery, although I was already quite dejected, the horrible sight of trees half-veiled by fog and prickly with icicles rent my heart again. How can I express

11 Michelet seeks out his classmate, Hector Poret (c. 1798–1864), with whom he had become close in 1813; they remained lifelong friends. They competed in the same *agrégation* examination (Poret won first place, Michelet third), but they helped each other throughout their academic careers. Poret was a respectable, though undistinguished, Hellenist who first taught at the Collège Charlemagne and then at the Collège Henri IV.

everything I thought about as we slowly walked along that doleful path? But what devastated me was the sound of the earth dropping upon the coffin. That wounded my heart with agonizing pain.

All three of us returned to the rue Popincourt, where my friend left us. At home, I could find only harsh words to say, both for others and for myself. I said to Pauline when I returned: "Your friend now has six feet of earth upon his heart."

27 February 1821, Tuesday

I had as much earth on mine, I believe, when I wrote this last Wednesday. Quite fortunately, I did not have time to continue, because I was extremely upset when I wrote that account, even more violently than on the very day of my misfortune. I could not eat until Friday. So I will not detail everything that followed. I will mention only the principal facts until I can elaborate all this in a small book about my friend.

Friday, the sixteenth, I went to the cemetery; but I had not taken the number of the grave with me, and I could not find it. I went down to the caretaker's lodge. But since my uncertainty about the location was not resolved, my sadness greatly diminished. Near me several people were readying a tombstone; this diverted me more. I went to the faubourg du Temple, where I thought his mother was. She had returned home; I found her already stronger. I went to the île Saint-Louis to inform the new tenant that we would remove Poinsot's belongings. I took care of that the next day and packed everything with the help of Poinsot's successor. I took the papers I had promised to Poret, gave them to him, and brought back the precious little note-book.

Sunday, the eighteenth, I went to the cemetery, dug out of the frozen ground a rather large number of stones, which I piled on the grave. In the middle, I placed a dry branch, which I decked with my two wreaths, red and white. Thus, his first monument was erected by my hands. I went to Poret's house and discussed the epitaph with him. I went home at three o'clock and Lefebvre[12] did not come. I was horrified by this. The next day, I went to Mme Poinsot's house to discuss the tombstone; and from there I left with her son to check the prices of several stones at the marble cutter's. Upon returning, I found the young Mme Fourcy, Lise, and Mlle Magry, who were dining at home.

Tuesday, Mme Poinsot and her cousin came to visit.

Wednesday, the twenty-first, I went to the Père-Lachaise cemetery and, on my return, I wrote in my *Journal* about the cruel event of the other Wednesday.

Thursday, the twenty-second, I went to the Bibliothèque du Roi.[13] M. Dacier had acceded to my request and had sent his servant with me to deliver his recommendations to M. Van Praet. I didn't find M. Dussault in and slipped a card under the door. (...)[14]

Friday, the twenty-third, I wrote Poret that I was not well enough to go and see him. He came, but late. Together we went to examine the sketch of the tomb inscription.

Saturday, the twenty-fourth, I finished taking notes from the second volume of De Gérando, and I took three pills. Sunday the twenty-fifth, I stayed at home and worked with great zeal. Monday even more: I began the *Departure of the Athenians* in Thucydides![15]

Today, Tuesday, the twenty-seventh, this morning, I went to the headmaster's house. On the rue de Jouy I ran into Chardin, who almost suffocated me in his embrace. From there to M. Villemain,

12 Michelet's first cousin, Paul Lefebvre-Millet, who was studying in Paris. He came from Renwez, the village of Michelet's maternal relations, in the Ardennes region of France.

13 Renamed the Bibliothèque nationale after the 1789 Revolution.

14 This means that part of the manuscript was missing and thus not in the French edition.

15 *Peloponnesian War*, book 6, chaps. 30–32.

whom I did not find at home. From there to M. Patinot and his son,[16] whom I found. Finally, to a reading room, where I read two newspapers until eleven o'clock.

28 February 1821, Wednesday

On a rather beautiful day I went to the cemetery and, from there, to Poret's house. Mlle Poinsot was waiting for me at home. She wanted me to take her to the Père-Lachaise. There was no way to refuse. On the way there we continuously spoke about her brother and her family. But, even though I still loved as usual the woman I should love,[17] I considered myself lucky to be alone with a pleasant woman under that beautiful sky. I felt that only vaguely, because my thoughts were, moreover, very pure and even solemn. I escorted her to the corner of the slaughterhouses, rue des Amandiers.[18]

– Michelet's true mourning was delayed. It took a full week for him to recover his presence of mind. Then, on 21 February, he inaugurated his system of anniversary reflections. Reviewing the past week, he sensitively examined the evolution of his grief. His immediate reaction, on the day of Poinsot's death, had been to take refuge in hopes of immortality and to exaggerate the survivor's failings. Michelet separated the noble and corrupt aspects of their friendship and stressed that he was not present at Poinsot's farewell. Was his friendship less urgent than tutoring the Roussel boy and preparing for his examinations? Ambition had distracted him, and he paid the penalty of acute guilt. When his mother died he had been sleeping after completing his homework. Now he felt like a father who had abandoned his son. The historian was never free of his conflict between "love and work."

Yet writing seemed to soothe his broken heart as he struggled to reconcile his self-involvement with his altruistic principles. He began

16 Chardin was a former classmate of Michelet's at the Collège Charlemagne. See above, note 7, for Villemain. Patinot was one of the pupils Michelet tutored at the Briand Institute, as were Roussel and Bodin.

17 Pauline Rousseau, who lived with him on the rue de la Roquette.

18 The street is one entrance to the Père-Lachaise and leads to the center of Ménilmontant, in the north.

the *Journal* entry of 14 February "two steps" from Poinsot's lifeless form. A week later he elaborated the details of his vigil, at which the original writing took place. Why did Michelet dwell upon the eerie beauty of the corpse's face and deliberately touch the cold, earthen flesh? First of all, he needed to confirm Poinsot's death despite his strong wish to deny it. More important, I believe, Michelet worked desperately to revive himself, to snatch himself from the jaws of oblivion. He strived to "overcome the stupor that absorbed" him—the depression caused by intense sorrow—by stimulating his emotions. Convinced that he deserved to perish, Michelet magnified his pain and enjoyed it.

The *Journal* stated more appropriate causes for guilt, however, although the author rarely detected their true significance. First and foremost, Poinsot died calling the name of his absent companion. Then, even before the funeral ended, Michelet decided that Hector Poret would become "Poinsot's heir" to his heart. Although hardly noticing how easily he replaced the deceased, he felt compelled to atone. On 18 February he erected Poinsot's "first monument" with his own hands. He then sketched "a small book" about his friend. But by the twenty-second he had returned to his research at the Biblio thèque du Roi. Finally, he admitted that he was sexually excited by Poinsot's sister while they visited the grave on the twenty-eighth. The conscientious student succumbed to her charm and thus insulted her brother's memory. At one and the same time he betrayed Paul, his soul mate, and Pauline, his mistress! Writing the *Journal* lifted these "crimes" to the surface of his awareness.

Between February and April 1821, Michelet recorded almost daily walks in the cemetery, arduous study, and numerous visits to people who might advance his career. He prepared his theses on Locke and Plutarch and read for the *agrégation*. In the weeks that followed, Michelet's subconscious relived the trauma of Poinsot's death. Poret and work replaced the deceased during the day, but at night his image returned in anxiety dreams that warned the survivor not to forget.

12 April 1821, Thursday

Today, Bodin starts taking his lessons again. Lefebvre comes with a friend from Renwez. Papa, during dinner, spoke to us about Poret's reserve. He said: "Even if he confides little in Jules, he sets him a good example." Those words so vividly summoned up the one who used to tell me everything, and to whom I told all, that I almost wept. Poinsot is dead: that thought struck my mind in the terms I set down here.

In our walk yesterday, I related my dream to Poret in which I saved a girl sold by her mother to M. de Richelieu.[19] I did not relate the other dream, in which I thought I saw Poinsot alive in a coffin, his head up and smiling to reassure us, nor did I relate yet another in which I saw severed limbs in a crypt and was told that they were his. They said, pointing to a pale face under glass: "There is your friend's head." Never have I experienced so much pain and horror.

* * *

29 April 1821, Sunday

I took advantage of a moment when it was not raining to go to the cemetery. I had dreamt a lot about Poinsot: we were together, I don't know how, in a miserable garret, and I warmly offered him my services; he did not accept. To return to my walk in the cemetery, it never seemed as poetic to me. Those young leaves, those gentle lawns, all that voluptuous springtime full of life and love, and all that on top of graves! Nothing could be more poetic and more philosophical at the same time. I brought my friend a wreath of roses.

When I returned home, I wrote some Latin verses about what I had just seen. I finished Euripides' *Andromache;* I read some Claudius, and Lefebvre arrived around four o'clock. He had taken a vomitory medicine and seemed very weak. We played cards after dinner with Mme de Coslin, and I stupidly stayed until ten-thirty. When I was preparing for bed, I learned that Lefebvre was supposed to take the ladies to see the fireworks on Tuesday. My imagination grew despon-

---

19 Armand-Emmanuel de Plessis, duc de Richelieu (1766–1822), an ultra-Royalist minister under Charles X, participated in the condemnation of Marshal Ney and, in December 1821, was removed by the Chamber of Deputies because of his harsh reactionary policies. In August 1816, Michelet had been awarded prizes in French and Latin at the Institut de France in the presence of the duc de Richelieu.

dent and, since my stomach was nearly empty, I spent part of the night sleepless.

30 *April 1821, Monday*
Today, by daybreak, my illness had disappeared. I gave a short lesson to Pauline. That caused an argument and a reconciliation. Before dinner, I went to the faubourg Saint-Jacques to deliver my ration coupons.

1 *May 1821, Tuesday*
Second year of the *Journal.* [. . .]

* * *

12 *May 1821, Saturday*
How inferior real pleasures are to the promises of imagination!

13 *May 1821, Sunday*
(8:00 a.m.) This week can be summarized with one word: I worked. I cannot compose any more verses today. I leave for the Ecole polytechnique and M. Leclerc.

Today I worked on my *Journal* in order to write down immediately the dream I just had. In a rather large room, near which several pharmacology students were living, I saw my poor Poinsot. I asked him how he could be there since he had been buried and mourned? "After they placed me in the earth," he answered, "they soon dug a hole near me to bury another person; I was not dead and I escaped." He spoke a lot about the young people who were near us. He told me they were saying bad things about me. I answered: "If I were alone, and useless to Papa, I would care about what they say. But I cannot fight." After this completely incoherent conversation, I found myself—I don't know how—with Mme Poinsot, walking along some of the outer boulevards. She said to me: "Now let's go visit the spot where we think the dear child is buried." After that, I happened to be with Mme Fourcy and Victoire,[20] who were leaving the house where I had seen

20 Victoire was Mme Poinsot's "little cousin." Twenty years later, Michelet would become involved with a servant named Victoire.

Poinsot. That house had something magical about it which I cannot convey. When we left we were greeted by a rain and hail storm. We were afflicted as if we had lost Poinsot again. Such dreams, as disturbing as they may seem, are quite precious to me.

* * *

6 July 1821, Friday

I am reading Flotte.[21] One thing struck me pleasantly yesterday. At 6:00 a.m. I see a man carrying a backpack, but dressed neatly, who was walking arm in arm with two girls, one twelve years old, the other about sixteen. The respectable appearance of this man, probably their father, moved me. He was probably taking them out for the day. That deeply moved me. The older girl was dressed in mourning. I seemed to see the very image of poverty, of affliction, of love of work and of virtue. Oh! If Bernardin de Saint-Pierre could have seen such harmony![22]

I no longer recall which night of the other week I thought I saw Poinsot in a dream. It was in our courtyard, near the gateway. He passed before me like an arrow; he was even more slender than usual. I said to him: "Oh, my poor friend, I thought you were dead" (I remember perfectly this was my mind's impulse), and I burst into tears.

I went to the cemetery today. As I was leaving, I saw a very beautiful, very pretty woman, quite elegant, enter with a young man. That created an unpleasant dissonance with the sadness of the place, of the weather, and of my heart. Hey, Madam! What are you doing here? Why don't you disturb other places with your beauty? I had just visited Poinsot, and the spot where I assume Mama was buried. My heart remembered the tone of her voice when she told me: "I love you

21 An accredited philosophy manual by J. S. Flotte, *Leçons élémentaires de philosophie, destinées aux élèves qui aspirent au grade de bachelier ès lettres* (1812; new edition, 1819).

22 Rousseau's disciple, Bernardin de Saint-Pierre (1737–1814), whose moral tales—entitled *Harmonies of Nature* (1815)—treat everyday events as examples of universal principles.

very much." My God, why this cruel friendship between men? *Siccine dividit amara mors.* [Thus bitter death divides.][23]

As I crossed that sad valley, I read on a tombstone: *To the memory...* The gravediggers had almost buried the monument. Other tombs, half-ruined, seemed about to disappear; the fences were collapsing. It seemed that only the trees wanted to protect them. I really like the saying: *The earth, our mother.*[24]

* * *

12 August 1821, Sunday

Today I am writing this sitting on my friend's tombstone. May the memory of his rectitude benefit my heart. I notice that I am exactly the same as I was last year, as feeble in my good resolutions, that is, equally corrupt. Oh, my friend, if only you could be with me right now, you who showed so much compassion for foolishness that you didn't share! My heart is very weak and very ill and doesn't know in whom to confide. Oh, dear friend, what has become of you? I wish that your tomb would speak! Why can't pure spirits communicate with us?

How can I convey my anxiety? How often, those days, cowardly, I wished to be completely unprincipled! Each time I experience this cruel state, these words appear to my mind in all their cruelty: "Poinsot is dead."

Last week passed like an unpleasant dream. Nothing more painful than that state. Pauline recently told me something striking: "If you are not happy like me, it is because you don't have peace of soul."

HISTORY AS MOURNING

–Grief gradually nurtured Michelet's desire to write history. Three dreams, recounted in the entry of 12 April, anticipated the historian's

---

23 The first appearance of this phrase in Michelet's writings. He will incorporate it in the epitaph of his wife's tomb in 1839.

24 This expression (in Latin, *terra mater*) will obsess Michelet the naturalist. See the Epilogue of this book.

prophetic calling. He allowed himself to tell Poret only the one that advertised his ideals, the dream in which he "saved a girl sold by her mother to M. de Richelieu," a Royalist tyrant to the liberal students. Twenty-five years later, as interpreter of the French Revolution, he would again redress such injustices. Michelet did not trust Poret with the two dreams in which Poinsot confronted him, nor with those of 29 April, 13 May, and 6 July, which also advertised his guilt. Michelet's subconscious both denied Poinsot's death and condemned the living friend's victory.

Michelet began to resolve these conflicts in his entry of 6 July by emulating Bernardin de Saint-Pierre. The poor laborer who bravely mothered his bereaved daughters (a stand-in for himself) symbolized the family he lacked. Less exalted needs also plagued him. When an attractive young couple "desecrated" the cemetery with displays of affection, Michelet blamed them instead of admitting that his own lust diverted him. The son's fragile fidelity to his mother and Poinsot unmasked his excessive self-absorption.

Michelet also began to appreciate how the Père-Lachaise fed his imagination; he was strangely inspired by mortality and decay: "all that voluptuous springtime full of life and love, and all that on top of graves! Nothing could be more poetic and more philosophical at the same time." Mourning released the energy to write verse or melodic prose and prompted him to invent ambitious systems.

Bereavement made an historian of the poet. His creative system challenged death. The mourner first reawakened his love for what he had lost; his memory focused upon the ideal and magnified it. Then the writer rendered the imagined past in beautiful prose. Michelet developed this esthetics of sorrow in the *Journal*. On 14 February he had begun by writing to Poinsot's corpse; on 12 August he continued on his very tombstone.

More than a month passed, however, before the budding historian began to draft his friend's life story; and it took still another loss to make him act. On 22 September he learned that Poret, not he, had been awarded first place in the *agrégation*. Only then did Michelet resolve to immortalize Poinsot. By preserving his "precious vestiges," Michelet's first historical essay will resurrect the past.

27 September 1821, Thursday
It was on 14 February this year that death stole my friend, from whom death alone could separate me. Soon afterward, I conceived the project of carefully collecting the innumerable memories of him that remained. Although most of them are indelibly printed in my heart, some events might slip my mind and, since nothing could compensate this forgetting, the years would have deprived me of some of those precious vestiges of my friend. Moreover, even if this collection were to be useless, I would nonetheless have undertaken it: first, to enjoy still something that can no longer recur; then, to preserve something of the memory of a very good and very virtuous man whom no one knew except me. This last desire remains quite vague in my mind, because this collection will never see the light of day (at least, through my doing) and because I do not intend to do anything worth showing. One person, at the most, should read this. I will dwell on everything; everything here is of equal worth... Such was my project, when the opening of the *agrégation* competition gave me hope of entering the university and caused me to defer its realization. I hesitated at first, wondering whether I shouldn't write this commentary before beginning the preparations necessary for the examinations. After much reflection, I believed I should wait, although it would cost me something. It even seemed to me that my friend would want me to do so if he had any sense of my dilemma. It was, by far, the most acute deprivation the examination imposed upon me.

I took the examination and, if I succeeded at all, only one of my friends will congratulate me. At least I am free, and I will first use my freedom to preserve that frail part of himself that Poinsot left behind, his memory. Surely such an upright person, good and considerate for twenty years, still lives somewhere other than in the memory of the one he loved. So take patience and hope. Never have I believed as strongly in God's justice and in our immortality.

Poinsot was born on 2 June 1798, and so his life lasted twenty-two years and eight and one-half months. I will divide this space of time into five periods, the last four of which were filled with our friendship, which includes more than ten years of his life. The first period lasted until he began studying with M. Mélot; the second until his return from Melun; the third until his reading of *Paul and Virginie*,[25] which produced a personal revolution in him; the fourth until the time he came to live with me; the fifth until his death. When I fill these five periods with all I remember, in orderly fashion, I will then add, at random, anything else I can find.

Poinsot was born at no. 67, rue Culture Sainte-Catherine.[26] His father, I believe, was still a cooper. Both sides of his family were wine growers from Vermanton, a village in Burgundy, near Auxerre. The husband was a tireless, hard worker, but knowing neither to read nor to write, he remained completely uncultured. The wife was more refined, clever; but she gained little, I believe, from greater contact with society. I think that Poinsot was a lot like his father.

His godparents were M. Geoffroy, a rich horse merchant with whom he maintained contact for the rest of his life, and Mme Coquart, mother or at least relative of two of my private pupils at the Briand Institute. He was given the name Paul, as his sister, shortly after, was named Virginie. Several associations make me pause on this name. It is the one he gave me when he became my godfather. Paul was also the character of Bernardin de Saint-Pierre, who caused a remarkable revolution in him, the great event of his life about which I should speak. And I believed that he himself embodied the simple and virtuous nature that the author attributes to the young Creole.

His mother placed him with a nursemaid in Burgundy, at Sens,

---

25 An immensely popular novel by Bernardin de Saint-Pierre, published in 1787 and a best seller in Michelet's time. *Paul et Virginie* recounts the sentimental story of two fatherless children brought up in savage innocence on the tropical island of Mauritius. Virginie drowns as Paul watches, and he dies two months later of a broken heart.

26 Now the rue de Sévigné in the Marais district of Paris.

because she was occupied with her business. He remained there until he was three years old. I don't know anything about that first period of his life. I only know that when he returned he was frail, and he remained more slender than sturdy. His brother told us that he often lost his fights with the workmen's little boys, while his brother, two or three years younger, pursued and fought them.

During that time, he was going to school at a M. Simane's. His handwriting then began to resemble his sister Virginie's, to such an extent that, when I recently saw some words that Virginie wrote after her brother's death, I shuddered despite myself. At nine years old, he was sent to board at Corbeil, and he remained there until he was twelve. Perhaps it was this separation, this first removal from the paternal home, that caused his predisposition to the melancholy that made him so interesting in his youth, but which perhaps impaired his constitution and shortened his life. He already needed to love someone. He sought friends at his boarding school; and what really is to his credit, I think, is that the two he found never entirely lost contact with him. Six weeks before his death, M. Potonier visited him at Saint-Louis. And, shortly after we lost him, M. X... of Essonne came to see Papa, who had once helped him to buy a guitar, following the advice of Poinsot, then at the Charité hospital. [. . .]

–Michelet unconsciously identified with the origins of Poinsot's personality, his own "predisposition to the melancholy that made him so interesting in his youth." Their bodies seemed to copy their minds. Like Poinsot, Michelet was short, small-boned, frail, and inclined to express internal conflicts through psychosomatic ills. The incipient historian believed that the absence of Poinsot's mother made him both thin and emotionally vulnerable. He sensed that Poinsot's early separation from loved ones established his particular insecurity, his inordinate need to love someone (or to be loved), but he could not penetrate the full significance of his intuition. (It was formerly believed that what happened to a child before the age of reason—that is, before the advent of speech—did not matter.) A quick rereading of the entry might have pointed Michelet to the truth: boarding school was *not* Poinsot's first separation from his family. Like numerous Parisian middle-class infants, he had been sent to a nursemaid in the country until the age of three. Apparently he had been badly cared for. Michelet understood obscurely that both he and his dearest friend suffered a maternal void.

MARRIAGE AND PROFESSIONAL SUCCESS (1821–1834)

The bereaved young man quickly became an adult after he stopped composing the *Memorial* in 1822. At age twenty-four, he had his *agrégation* in hand and enjoyed a permanent position teaching philosophy and history at the Collège Sainte-Barbe, one of Paris's leading secondary schools. His intimate life was also eventful. His godmother, Mme Fourcy, died in December 1823, at the age of fifty-six. Michelet had lost more than another mother. He was liberated from the conflict of a dual intimacy: with his *bonne maman* and his younger mistress. Pauline became pregnant around the time of Mme Fourcy's death, and Michelet finally married her on 20 May 1824, after she had carried their child six months. A daughter, Adèle, was born on 28 August of that year. Their only other child, Charles, was born on 12 November 1829.

Michelet pursued a brilliant career. In 1824 he met the influential philosopher Victor Cousin (1792–1867), one of the Restoration's most charismatic writers and lecturers. Michelet began to publish pedagogical history manuals to increase his visibility, and his efforts were soon rewarded. In January 1827 he was named professor of philosophy and history at the Ecole normale, the elite school that formed the nation's finest teachers. Michelet's groundbreaking translation and interpretation of Vico's *Principles of the Philosophy of History*[27] appeared in March of that year. In April 1827 Michelet moved with his father, wife, and daughter to the rue de l'Arbalète. To further his knowledge,

---

27 In *Principles of a New Science Concerning the Common Nature of Nations,* Giambattista Vico (1668–1744) defined the natural laws governing historical development.

he left France for the first time to visit scholars and consult libraries in Germany, from 6 August to 18 September 1828. By age thirty, Michelet had proven himself as a distinguished writer, researcher, and professor.

His accomplishments were also rewarded by the ruling family of the Restoration. In September 1828 he began tutoring Marie-Thérèse, princesse de Berry, the nine-year-old granddaughter of the king, Charles X. But Michelet welcomed the revolution that broke out in July 1830. He was not a bold radical but an ambivalent revolutionary who deplored violence and yearned for social stability. The July Revolution inspired him with a vision of France unified, and he was quick to cooperate with the new constitutional monarchy. He was appointed tutor of Princess Clémentine, age thirteen, the daughter of Louis-Philippe. Michelet was clearly a friend of the powers that be.

His career was guaranteed. In October 1830 he was named head of the historical section of the Royal Archives (which later became the National Archives). In April 1831 he published his philosophical manifesto, *Introduction to Universal History*, which pictured the progress of mankind as an epic battle of freedom versus determinism. History was the drama of a collective humanity, led by men of genius, liberating its mind from the shackles of matter. France was like a single person progressively freeing itself from the constraints of race, geography, and regional character. This "person" reached fulfillment in the Revolution of 1789. Then followed a period of decadence, the nineteenth century.

Michelet applied his philosophy of history to concrete facts about the origins of modern France. He uncovered original documents in the Archives. At the Ecole normale he developed courses on medieval history. His *History of the Roman Republic* had appeared in July 1831. By December 1833 the first two volumes of his monumental *History of France* went on sale. The author identified himself as France's historian who admired a nonorthodox spiritual ideal of the Catholic Middle Ages.

The Journal. Nothing remains of Michelet's youthful *Journal* between 1823 and 1828. Did his publications and multiple teaching duties dominate his inner life? Or was that the part of the diary destroyed by his second wife, Athénaïs, who wanted to diminish the memory of her predecessor, Pauline? Michelet's succinct summaries of his research and reflections, however, did survive: notebooks that he entitled *Journal of Ideas* (written from 1821 to October 1829) and *Journal of My Readings* (1818–April 1829). The private *Journal* shows no evidence of his self-explorations until 1834.

Michelet had become a university professor by the beginning of 1834, temporarily replacing Guizot[28] in the chair of modern history at the Sorbonne. He continued to savor his walks in the Père-Lachaise cemetery that became a meditative center. He would stalk among its monuments pondering his nation's past, mindful of loved ones buried within its walls, and elaborating parallels between French history and his own experience.

Autobiography and interpretation of his nation indeed began to merge. The 1834 entries reveal Michelet's unique mixture of historical and intimate concerns; they are like prose poems that orchestrate the themes of loss and love. For the first time we feel the energetic pulse-beat of his mature prose. His style gains power from the personal grief that motivates his dreams of literary resurrection of the dead.

The *Journal*'s great historical panoramas begin on 4 May 1834, when Michelet will celebrate the fourteenth anniversary of Poinsot's residency at Bicêtre (and the inception of the *Journal*) by visiting the cemetery with his ten-year-old daughter. Memories of lost friendship and sexual desire awaken at the graves of Poinsot and one of his sisters: defensively, Michelet avoids dwelling upon Sophie Plateau, his first passionate infatuation,[29] and, significantly, he cannot find Mme Fourcy's grave.[30] Only political heroes compensate for his dearth of companionship. The memory of Georges Farcy (1800–30), a poet and

28 François Guizot (1787–1874) was professor of modern history at the Sorbonne from 1812 to 1830. His political career began after the Restoration when he helped found the Doctrinaires, the party that favored the constitutional monarchy. He was minister of education between 1832 and 1837. See below, note 42.

29 See Prologue, note 9.

30 In vol. 5 of the *History of France* (book 7, chap. 1), Michelet explains her epitaph, *Hinc surrectura!* [From here she will arise!], in a footnote: "That inscription, perhaps the most beautiful that could be found on a Christian grave, was placed by my friend M. Fourcy (librarian of the Ecole polytechnique) on his mother's tombstone."

philosopher killed in the July Revolution, generates the following epic vision.

4 May 1834, Sunday

At the Père-Lachaise with my daughter. Anniversary of the day I went to see Poinsot at Bicêtre in 1820. I found the tombs of Poinsot and his sister.[31] I could not find Mme Fourcy (*hinc surrectura!* [from here she will arise!]) or Farcy, for whom I searched in vain among the fighters of the July Revolution. I did not look for Sophie Plateau, I would not have found her.

Scaffolding of the July monument, alongside the plaster elephant that melts in the rain: precocious decay of the great Empire![32]

For this necropolis of a godless era in the shape of an amphitheater, for this city of the dead facing the city of the living, I believe I can already distinguish three periods of its short history:

1.—The Empire: I have seen the old, little house which was already there before that era. I have walked the worn steps where the century of Louis XIV had passed (see my *Journal* of 1821). Then Delille, the Clary family, then the generals Kellermann, Suchet, Masséna, the atheists Volney, Monge.[33]

---

31 I have not been able to ascertain which sister died and when.

32 Napoleon had ordered a bronze statue of an elephant erected in the southeast corner of the place de la Bastille. A monument to the July Revolution, which still stands, was under construction in 1834. The plaster model of the bronze statue, which Michelet considered to be a symbol of the emperor's fragile glory, was never completed and was removed in 1846. Gavroche, in Victor Hugo's novel, *Les Misérables* (1862), lives inside the plaster beast.

33 Napoleon's Empire (1804–14) is represented by the neoclassical poet and translator of Virgil and Milton, the abbé Jacques Delille (1738–1813). The rich merchant Clary married his daughter Julie to Joseph Bonaparte and his daughter Désirée to Bernadotte. Napoleon's heroic marshals of the Empire are memorialized by François-Christophe Kellermann (1735–1820), Louis-Gabriel Suchet (1770–1826), and André Masséna (1758–1817). Two thinkers represent modern secularism: Constantin, comte de Volney (1757–1820), important author of *Voyage to Syria and Egypt* (1787) and *Ruins; or, Meditations on the Revolution of Empires* (1791); and the physicist and geometrician Gaspard Monge (1746–1818), who founded the national engineering school, the Ecole polytechnique.

2.—The Restoration begins with Labédoyère. Next the chapel, aristocratic and romantic tomb of Mme de Duras. Next General Foy: a slightly theatrical monument, but which is perhaps all the more patriotic because of it.[34]

3.—Since the July Revolution, extension outward of the cemetery: martyrs, simple and pure people (Farcy), political men who died in pain (Lamarque, Périer).[35]

It was right to place Abélard's tomb here.[36] That precursor of

---

34 The Restoration of the Bourbon dynasty after the fall of Napoleon began in 1814 and lasted until the 1830 revolution. Michelet associates its inception with the emperor's former general, Charles-Angélique-François Labédoyère (1786–1815), who briefly joined forces with Louis XVIII and then welcomed Napoleon back from his Elba exile in 1815, when he was commander of the garrison at Grenoble. After Napoleon's defeat at Waterloo, Labédoyère returned to Paris, quite deliberately, where he was executed. Claire Lechat de Kersaint, Mme de Duras (1778–1828), hosted a brilliant salon during the Restoration and published two very successful novels that promoted social equality. The liberal general Maximilien-Sébastien Foy (1775–1825) was a celebrated political orator. After 1819 he recalled the lost glories of Napoleon's Republic and Empire. A national subscription helped erect a magnificent monument sculpted by David d'Angers. The principal figure shows General Foy in the toga of a Roman senator. See below, entry of 18 March 1838.

35 The July Monarchy (1830–48) incarnated Michelet's hope of national renewal and equality. Georges Farcy (see above) died in the July battles. The general and political orator Maximilien Lamarque (1770–1832) had suppressed a rebellion for Napoleon in the Vendée region and retired after his fall. In 1828 he returned to public life and led the liberal opposition to the Restoration and the July Monarchy. A republican insurrection broke out after Lamarque was buried on 1 June 1832. Michelet will return to the imposing tomb of the statesman and banker Casimir Périer (1777–1832). He was legendary for his ferocious temper and violent language in public sessions of the legislature during the Restoration. When the July Revolution broke out, after much hesitation, Périer supported Louis-Philippe. Several eminent doctors could not decide whether Périer died of cholera or brain disease. A fifty-page case history was published in the Paris *Gazette médicale*. The city of Paris erected an impressive, if vulgar, monument to one of its most colorful figures.

36 Pierre Abélard (1079–1142) was revered for his tragic love affair with the nun Héloïse (1101–64), a former pupil who gave birth to their child. They were separated after Abélard was castrated by hired thugs. Héloïse became the head of the convent of the Paraclete and exchanged a correspondence with her lover, who ended his life in the monastery of Cluny. Their remains were transferred to the Père-Lachaise cemetery in 1815, where they are consecrated by a lovely monument in the form of a Gothic chapel.

modern rationalism appropriately belongs at the center of this cemetery. He is at the center of his victory there. The only religion displayed on his tomb—I was going to say, his Gothic temple—is a religion of nature, of sensual nature, epitomized by woman.

Alongside, the Jewish cemetery.

18 May 1834, Sunday of Pentecost

A view of Paris from the heights of Ménilmontant, sometimes visible, other times hidden. Poor old Rousseau was knocked down on this hill by the Great Dane of M. Lepelletier Saint-Fargeau.[37] It was there, behind the Père-Lachaise, behind Saint-Cricq's garden, where my brother-in-law died,[38] near the walnut tree where I lingered with Pauline in 1818 (stormy day); there, I say, is where Rousseau took his reverie for a walk. Several years later his books ruled France.

All of France's celebrities of the last thirty years are crammed together on the southern side of the same hill. At the bottom, Bernardin de Saint-Pierre, Parny, Monge. In the middle of the hill, Delille, Laplace, Grétry and generals Kellermann, Masséna, Lefebvre, Gouvion-Saint-Cyr.[39] At the top, General Foy, the military orator, the eloquent spokesman for the army; he represents the opposition under the Restoration, the national protest. Behind, hidden from view,

---

37 Allusion to an incident recounted by J.-J. Rousseau in *Reveries of a Solitary Walker* (1782), second *promenade.*

38 Pauline's half-brother, Guillaume de Navailles (born in 1783), died in 1833, one year after his mother. Michelet was (appropriately) convinced that he lived in an incestuous relationship with his mother, the baronne de Navailles, only fifteen years his senior. He had lived near the Père-Lachaise in a house owned by Auguste de Saint-Cricq, a poet who translated the *Fables* of Phaedrus.

39 Michelet reviews the Empire and the Restoration. Names not covered in previous notes: Evariste-Désiré de Parny (1753–1814) was the renowned author of elegiac love poetry. The composer André-Ernest-Modeste Grétry (1741–1813) was famous for his comic operas. Pierre-Simon, marquis de Laplace (1749–1827) was a celebrated mathematician and astronomer who became minister of the interior during Napoleon's Consulate and senator during the Empire. François-Joseph Lefebvre (1755–1820) and Laurent Gouvion-Saint-Cyr (1764–1830) are two more of Napoleon's marshals of the Empire.

against the enclosing wall, the pyramid of Volney, critic and misanthrope.

Paris undulates with remarkable grace when seen from there. It flows with the Seine from the green hillocks of Saint-Mandé and Yvry, through Saint-Paul, Notre-Dame, the Louvre, and the Arc de Triomphe. In the distance, the gilded dome of the Invalides and, rising above everything, the triumphant bulk of the Panthéon. Notre-Dame is in the center. Behind it, the old Paris of the Marais. Beyond is the vast modern Paris, which develops and strives toward the Arc de Triomphe.

Green at Vincennes, stormy at the Panthéon, dusty at the Arc de Triomphe and the Père-Lachaise, where roses hide its marble tombs. From time to time, the powerful voice of the nightingale...

* * *

20 July 1834, Sunday

If I decide sooner or later (and it will be later) to summarize the memories of my individual existence, that period of my life when I did not yet live the general life, I shall take as its center, its text, its theater, the Père-Lachaise cemetery. That entire period of my life (1815–25) from my mother's death to those of Mme Fourcy and Poinsot, to my marriage, my essays on Vico, to my discourse on the unity of science[40]—that entire period, I say, developed within a narrow radius, between the Marais, the Jardin des Plantes, Bicêtre, Vincennes, the Père-Lachaise. There took place my loves, walks with friends, my losses, my regrets... The first events of my life could be set there as episodes. They would be memorials, but partially freed from the pettiness of individual life. At least that individuality would fuse with all the great individuals of the period, in this awesome theater of life

40 Michelet delivered his "discours sur l'unité de la science" at the Collège Sainte-Barbe on 17 August 1825. This profession of faith sets forth a pedagogical system and philosophical method, the goal of which is a total knowledge of human culture. His translation of Vico appeared in 1827.

and death, where tombs are framed by roses, where silence alternates with nightingales, mourning with love.

The young man's individual passions would become less trivial if played out upon those great tombs... His personal passions would assume something grandiose and philosophical in contrast with a place at once so charming and so tragic. An eloquent biography of our most illustrious contemporaries would be interwoven with that of the author, and both would be contained within the great biography of nature... It would be at once art, history, and philosophy.

Could not the author's life even advance, and to a certain extent progress, alongside of individual and general events? Thus, with each loss, the author would step farther beyond mere individuality. He would thus expand himself at the same time as the public spirit expanded during the Restoration. His strength would burst forth as did France after the July Revolution. He began his abundant production during that period. Finally, detached little by little from every local bond, he would inaugurate his traveling and European existence. [. . .]

AUTOBIOGRAPHY, HISTORY, AND RESURRECTION (1834–1838)

– Michelet continued to teach at the Ecole normale until 1836, and he lectured successfully while advancing his writing projects. He traveled to collect material for his courses and books. Abundant and detailed observations fill the *Journal* of his trip to England from 5 August to 5 September 1834. Another important voyage, this time to Aquitaine, the southwest of France, lasting from 18 August to 25 September 1835, helped prepare volume 3 of the *History of France* and his ethnographic study of medieval law and folk customs, *The Origins of French Law, Studied in the Symbols and Formulas of Universal Law*. Both books appeared in June 1836.[41]

[41] Only one *Journal* entry remains for the entire year 1836. The following year, before his trip to Belgium and Holland (23 June–18 July), includes only one entry per month. Each is significant. See below, References, for problems of dating.

Michelet further refined his historical method as he continued to mourn Poinsot. His grief persisted over the sixteen years after Poinsot's death and became part of his thinking. He systematized his merger of history and autobiography by formulating a sophisticated theory of the artist's multiple selves in the entry of 7 February 1837: the individual man, as a "self," becomes "symbolic" of the "multiple nonself" who sees himself in the collective personhood of his nation. However, the author retains his freedom through esthetic distance: He is variously a man of flesh and blood (called "my individual self"), an artist ("my literary self"), and a prophet or judge ("my moral self"). Michelet could control his life more effectively by separating his various functions—but his inner integrity suffered. How could the writer harmonize self-absorption and altruistic ideals?

7 February 1837, Tuesday of Lent

Walk through my cemetery of the doctrine.[42] Cold and beautiful spring-winter day.

Shouldn't the individual be symbolic of the collectivity? Thus I am part of a multiple nonself that will appear through my death. The dissolving of the individual dissipates life so that it will flourish in more varied and more beautiful forms. Thus it is a substitute mirror of condensed life...

We progress from one ideal to a more complex ideal, for example, from Saint-Louis to the Maid of Orleans.[43] *Sic* [ditto] in the life of society. But also in individual existences: I pass from my individual self to my literary self, which intensifies the world as beauty, then to my moral self, which absorbs the world as benevolence, so that it may purify itself through resignation...

---

42 "The doctrine, a political system under the Restoration that, attempting to reconcile the monarchy with freedom, sought to realize this by defining a system of political dogmas" (Littré dictionary). The Doctrinaires formed a small but influential political party led by Pierre-Paul Royer-Collard (1763–1845) and François Guizot. They represented an ideology of moderation (the *juste-milieu*) and supported a constitutional monarchy.

43 Joan of Arc, heroine of the common people; see *History of France*, vol. 5, published 23 August 1841.

Oh! May I at least be able to follow that path and improve myself by going from self to self. But my habit of seeking a result, an outward result, prevents me...

* * *

June 1837 (without specific date)
Carrel's dream;[44] premonition, the night before his duel. He did not even draw back in face of his adversary. Premonitions of Rabbe; that Cyclops died alone, for his mistress had fled with his boot polisher. In the desertion of his final moments, having lost his mistress and his dog, he sent for Carrel, who sat up with him. Rabbe said to him, an hour before he died: "Amédée Thierry told me. 'I am beginning to see, my ideas are becoming clearer. There is something to which I go. One must watch it when alive...'"

Compare with the dying Abel Rémusat to whom Saint-Martin dared not speak about his soul; but he left the *Phaedo* on his bed (E. Burnouf).

22 June 1837, Thursday
Adèle's first communion, the eve of my departure for Holland. Marvelous celebration. The veil: she seemed to be a woman. The girls sang alone. Sweetness and power of that crowd's voice, so touched with emotion and so pure. The little boys watch without understanding.

–Michelet left for Belgium and Holland on 23 June to research volume 4 of the *History of France*. But the *Journal* reveals a chaotic anxiety as the historian began to perceive his long-hidden impulse to destroy himself. The dreams he records of other men almost make his death wish conscious. The undated entry of June 1837 played out his

44 The allusions are explained in the commentary that follows.

internal drama through notorious victims of his time. The well-known political journalist Armand Carrel (born 1800) was shot by the newspaper editor Emile de Girardin (1806–81) in a duel motivated by an ideological dispute. Carrel died on 22 July 1836. Michelet associated that recent tragedy with another celebrated quasi suicide, that of the historian and journalist Alphonse Rabbe (born 1776). Rabbe was a depressed man, horribly disfigured by syphilis; when he died of an overdose of laudanum on 1 January 1830, a legend was born.[45] Michelet then linked Rabbe with the historian Amédée Thierry (1797–1873), brother of the more influential Augustin Thierry. These deceased young men of promise seem to solicit Michelet from beyond the grave.

The historian approached these deaths in a scholarly manner. He compared the ones that resulted from personal discord with the death of the Orientalist Abel Rémusat (born 1788), who perished in the 1832 cholera epidemic. Michelet's friend, professor of Sanskrit at the Collège de France, Eugène Burnouf (1801–52), who had studied under Rémusat, apparently told him that his professor had died while reading Plato's dialogue on immortality, the *Phaedo,* which dramatizes the self-destruction of Socrates. Could the historian imitate the sage, recover his poise, and accept life and death with equanimity?

Domestic strife also tormented him. He saw himself as a derelict husband, plagued by inner solitude and guilt. As he admired his daughter's first communion, he identified with the little boys who watched the girls without feeling their singing faith. He worshiped the ideal of family but compromised it all too often. Preoccupied with his own career, he left his wife, Pauline, to fend for herself. He acknowledged their estrangement in letters to her soon after leaving Paris. On 24 June he wrote: "My dear wife, I left with the sad feeling of your reproaches. I have never had a sadder departure." Pauline would die two years later.

The *Journal* of 1838, in the Viallaneix edition, begins only with June, and features the rich account of Michelet's trip to Switzerland and

[45] Victor Hugo dedicated a poem against suicide (no. 17) to Rabbe in *Chants du crépuscule* (1835).

northern Italy. Accompanied by the young Frédéric Baudry,[46] the historian undertook this important research to document the wars of Italy and his history of Louis XII. The voyage lasted from 8 July to 17 August.

Before his departure, however, Michelet began a peculiar but (for him) fruitful ritual. Poinsot's family had finally decided not to renew the lease on his tomb, as most sites were not normally obtained in perpetuity. Michelet could witness his friend's exhumation. According to strict judicial procedures, Poinsot's mortal remains were to be disinterred and transported either to a public ossuary or to another grave. In March, Michelet will note a visit to the Père-Lachaise that revived the historical panoramas of 1834. Then in April, two days after he began his Collège de France course, an "Introduction to the History of France," he will complete his mourning for his treasured companion. This excavation will allow him to rehearse his powers of artistic resurrection.

18 March 1838, Sunday

At the Père-Lachaise with my daughter, the day of the dinner with Souvestre, between the Collège de France election and that of the Académie.[47] I have never seen this place so sad, despite the crowd. The entire space between the two walkways (Sophie Plateau, etc...) is torn up. Poinsot's plot is too, partially. I am even afraid something will happen to it (I must reach an understanding with his brother). His grave is neglected. His sister's seems less so, encircled by beautiful iron railings.

Those leafless trees, the white stones that rise up on all sides, everything seemed bare to me, sad and harsh, despite the softening hues of a half-shadow.

---

46 See below, chap. 3, n. 10.

47 Michelet was elected to the Collège de France on 8 January 1837 and on 23 April to the Académie des sciences morales et politiques. Emile Souvestre (1806–54) was a journalist from Brittany and author of numerous popular plays and novels.

Placed a wreath at the abandoned grave of B. Constant.[48] Abélard's tomb: the two statues seem less ancient than the bas-reliefs that encircle the stone. Proud tomb of C. Périer:[49] bas-reliefs heavy and weak in their execution; the statue is beautiful but hardly resembles him; in sum, worthy of that proud and irascible genius.

25 April 1838, Wednesday

Exhumation of Poinsot. At eight o'clock in the morning, said good-bye to Quinet,[50] who leaves for Lyon. From there to the house of Poinsot's brother on the rue Chabrol. His establishment maintains its animals by giving them what nature requires. The other dairies are nuns' convents. Poinsot's fat and industrious wife keeps the books, writes the letters; her husband seems too harsh and brusque for her. Pauline found her alone with her five children, while her husband was at Versailles.

The young, intelligent horse practically takes us of its own accord to the Père-Lachaise where it had, however, been only once before.

Exhumation, in the presence of the cemetery caretaker and the police official. The wood of the coffin has decayed, except for the board on the bottom. The silk lining and last artificial bouquet (leather orange blossoms) were completely preserved. Everything had taken the color of wood and earth. His skull seems enormous, larger than

48 Benjamin Constant (1767–1830), who had a stormy political career under Napoleon, wrote the psychological novel *Adolphe* (1807; first published, 1816) and during the Restoration was the leader of the liberal opposition. He sent his book *De la religion* (1824–26) to Michelet in 1828 after the latter's "discours sur l'unité de la science" was published in a Swiss review.

49 See above, note 35.

50 Michelet met his lifelong friend, Edgar Quinet (1803–75), at the home of Victor Cousin in May 1825. Cousin urged Quinet to translate Herder's *Ideen* and Michelet to translate Vico. Quinet wrote volumes on history, religion, and epic poems. He was professor of language and literature of southern Europe at the Collège de France, with Michelet, from 1842 to 1851, when he went into voluntary exile following Louis-Napoleon's *coup d'état.*

when he was alive: It is death's dignity, the true lasting monument that remains of man. All his teeth remained completely intact, beautiful, white... Apart from that, the bones were detached from one another, even the finger bones.

His skull and its empty eyes were not without beauty, perhaps because I placed back the gentle intelligence that had animated them and the hopes we held for this young and noble head... I placed a white wreath upon it.

2 My Wife's Death

PAULINE ROUSSEAU MICHELET
1792–24 July 1839

– She, in whom each evening you found self-forgetfulness and that intoxicating death of self called love. For me she was nature in its lively spontaneity, devoted to my individuality, beyond nature, against nature . . .

Everything together, then nothing together: It is dying more than if we both had died . . .
Journal, 12 September 1839 –

PAULINE'S EPITAPH

Paulina Rousseau-Michelet
Julii Michelet
Uxor.
Mater dilectissima II liberorum.
Aegrotantis quondam viri
Salus.
Levamen laborum.
Perpetua in utraque fortuna
Felicitas.

MDCCCXXXIX.

Siccine dividit amara
Mors.
Quousque Domine.

* * *

Beatus qui intelligit super egenum et pauperem.
In die mala liberabit eum
Dominus.

[Pauline Rousseau-Michelet
Wife of Jules Michelet.
Beloved mother of two children.
Salvation of her formerly sick husband.
She consoled him in his labors.
Constant felicity in good or evil fortune.

1839

Thus bitter death divides.
How long, O Lord.

* * *

Blessed is he who understands above the indigent and the poor.
He will liberate them from evil days.
Lord.]

A SUCCESSFUL CAREER (1837–1839)

–Two decades of arduous work earned Michelet the crown of his teaching career: his professorship at the Collège de France, the most prestigious academic pulpit of nineteenth-century France. He was elected in January 1838 and in April gave his inaugural lesson on the city of Paris. He held the chair of history and moral philosophy until the government suspended his course in March 1851 and eventually forced his resignation in 1852. His flamboyant lectures to amphitheaters crowded with enthusiastic youth established him as one of the era's most influential celebrities.

But the man's personal life was collapsing. He had married a woman who could never share his intellectual passions. Her lack of education distressed him, although he delighted in her sensuousness and was touched by the hardships she had endured. Pauline Rousseau was born in Paris in 1792, the illegitimate child of the baronne de Navailles and the Paris Opera tenor Jean-Joseph Rousseau.[1] Pauline's sufferings seemed to reflect those of her mother. At age fifteen, Claude-Oudette-Gilles Charles had married an elderly tubercular gentleman who gave her his title, a son,[2] and little else. Proud of her contracted nobility, the baroness did not obtain a birth certificate for Pauline. The daughter was neglected, sent away to board, and she finally entered the Ursuline convent school in Meaux, outside of Paris, in 1814. Fortunately, some women from the Scellier family befriended Pauline and helped her return to Paris to help care for an ailing and demented marquise. She then met the young Michelet at the sanitorium in which they lived and in 1818 began their relationship. They were married in 1824 when Pauline was six months pregnant.

Their marriage was one-sided, to say the least. Michelet was its absolute center and Pauline his devoted helper. He often ignored his wife while he wrote, studied, lectured, or traveled. Yet he did love her, remained faithful, sent her detailed, affectionate letters on his frequent trips—but considered her only as an appendage. She looked

1 Jean-Joseph Rousseau became famous around 1779 and died in 1800.

2 Guillaume-Girard-Judith de Navailles; see above, chap. 1, n. 38.

after the household and their two children; but even there, she had no real authority. Furcy Michelet, the historian's father, administered the family's finances, ran errands for his son, copied his manuscripts, and supervised his daughter-in-law's tasks. Jules enjoyed sexual relations with Pauline but usually slept in his father's bedroom. Over the years Pauline became increasingly despondent, grew obese, and took refuge in alcohol. After more than twenty years of cohabitation with Michelet (and fifteen as his wife), Pauline contracted tuberculosis and started to waste away. She died on 24 July 1839 at the age of forty-seven.

The important entry of January 1839—in which Michelet defined his autobiographical approach to writing history—will introduce this chapter. His cult of the cemetery had combined ethics and poetics: "Loving the dead is a form of immortality." Mourning developed the historian's genius, his "gift of tears"; compassion, a form of esthetic empathy, became his method. The erudite artist identified with the departed and quickened them with his own emotions.

January 1839

We were the same, he and I: an identity through compassion (*sic* Valmiki).[3]

If Pythagoras[4] remembered having been one of the commanders in the Trojan War, why couldn't I remember having been the destitute man who lived through ancient slavery, serfdom during the Crusades, the worker of modern times?

If all that is not me, I feel a true enough, immense enough compassion to shoulder all those woes.

The historian's harsh fate is to love, to lose so many things, to begin

---

3 Valmiki, considered in Michelet's time to be the father of Sanskrit poetry, was the author of the *Ramayana*, the great epic poem of ancient India. In *The People* (1846) Michelet will describe how the poet's sobbing for a slain dove engendered his rhythmic song (part 2, chap. 6).

4 Pythagoras was a Greek philosopher (c. 580–c. 500 B.C.E.) who proposed a theory of reincarnation used by many nineteenth-century poets and thinkers.

anew all the loves, all the bereavements of humanity. I have just read some of Petrarch's sonnets.[5] But how many sonnets and *canzoni* would I need to help me weep for so many aborted loves that my heart has endured across the centuries? (Translate sonnet 13.)

But what if those past passions relieve present ones! Since in the end everything must die, let us begin by loving the dead.

As we trace the development of the human race and its journey from one ideal to another one, more complete, we will probably place our own ideal high enough, so that henceforth anything can provoke our pity. Each individual, no matter how lofty, will henceforth appear too incomplete, and the present will neither threaten nor attract us. Thus may our souls sprout wings, and may the next journey go more easily! Loving the dead is a form of immortality.

* * *

[Pauline died on 24 July 1839.]

–Does the *Journal's* relative silence bear witness to Michelet's complicated grief or to the scissors of Athénaïs? What remains, in any case, testifies to Michelet's bitterly guilty love for his unfortunate first wife. Although Pauline's tuberculosis was advanced, he continued working at a feverish pace. Ambition and self-absorption had overpowered love: His mission expanded his ego. In two long autobiographical reflections (which we do not cite), those of February and 10 March 1839, he identified with Paris. The city of his birth was France's nerve center or *sensorium*, while the nation as a whole was Europe's brain. His wife's illness did not prevent him from visiting Auxerre, Autun, and Lyon, where he observed the dangers of industrialization. He started that trip on Palm Sunday, 24 March 1839, and

[5] Francesco Petrarca (1304–74) was an Italian poet and humanist whose poems inspired French Renaissance writers. Petrarch's Laura, like Dante's Beatrice, enabled the poet to express the conflict between earthly passions and divine love.

returned to Paris on 7 April. One month later, on 6 June, his dying wife entered a private clinic in Passy, outside of Paris. Only two entries (dated 23 June and 4 July) precede Pauline's death on 24 July. Immediately afterward, Michelet undertook a microscopic review of his bereavement.

Death forced the widower to face his moral frailty. Selfishly, he had neglected his wife, undermined her self-esteem, while he exploited her domestic skills and longing for affection. He had assuaged his lusts in Pauline's bed but had reserved for his father the tender communion of sleep. As a morally committed historian, his mission was to resurrect the shades, but deep within he felt feeble. His wife's death provoked a devastating crisis of faith, which he entrusted to the *Journal* one hour after she perished.

24 July 1839, Wednesday

9:00 a.m. My poor Pauline entered Meyer's clinic in Passy on 6 June 1839. She was already quite sick, but we did not suspect that her lungs were stricken. Her character had changed; she hid from me, she became a stranger. She wanted to receive only Mme Legendre; she took an aversion to Mme Guillaumont, M. Aupépin.[6] She was already dead to me, a cruel fact!

She left during a frightful storm, while thunderbolts fell across her path, at the dome of the Invalides. For more than two weeks she endured cold, rainy weather, or else bitter winds.

I visited there three times a week, usually crossing the museum on Sunday, and from Neuilly Wednesdays and Fridays. I walked from Porte Maillot to the Muette, a lovely road (especially on a day of impending storm; I noticed that). But most often I was too tired, too sad... From a laborious lecture, which had drained me, I walked along the dusty road between the carriages and the fashionable horsemen, I was going... where?... To meet death even in my poor

6 M. Aupépin was Michelet's family physician and close friend. The doctor's buxom wife and Michelet eventually became lovers.

little room... Did I say *mine*? In a rented room. From afar I would see my poor wife, each day thinner, paler, who from the small balcony watched me approach.

However, one positive aspect (cruel, too, in thinking about it), our hearts drew closer... probably to make the separation sadder, to increase the heartbreak.

Saturday, 13 July, in the evening, I brought M. Récamier there, who did not find her ill! MM. Aupépin, Baroilhet, Maurel, Trousset had unanimously given up on her.[7] Saturday, 20 July, I let my daughter come home for dinner, where we waited for Dargaud[8] and the little Maurel boy, Charles's playmate. During that time M. Aupépin visited Pauline, at my request. She told him that she thought she was finished... He thought she would die within forty-eight hours.

Sunday, M. Meyer gave me a small room in which to sleep, without her knowledge. Monday, Tuesday, I still returned to Paris. Tuesday morning, I went there at 4:00 a.m. and sent the maid to bed. From four to eight, Pauline and I remained hand in hand, looking into each other's eyes. She did not speak. But she made little nervous gestures, expressing discouragement like a pitiful child who tries to say that he feels himself dying. I tried not to let her see me cry. More than once, she squeezed my hand, and once she kissed me.

Tuesday, I rushed to Paris to entreat M. Aupépin and M. Maurel to come and delude her about her condition, if at all possible. M. Maurel went along with this with a kindness for which I will be forever grateful. M. Aupépin, perhaps more deeply touched, revealed all too clearly everything he thought by his gloomy expression.

---

7 All these men were doctors.

8 The writer and historian Jean-Marie Dargaud (1800–66) was introduced to Michelet in 1830 by their mutual friend, Edgar Quinet. Dargaud became closely associated in 1831 with the poet Alphonse de Lamartine (1790–1869), who became president of the provisional government for one year after the 1848 revolution. Dargaud remained close to both Michelet and Lamartine despite their increasing political differences.

These thoughts of impending death are quite dreadful for a pitiful woman who was so afraid of it. She who dared not remain alone, feeling that, solitary, she would die. Oh! It is too much, great God, alas! For we can do nothing more for her. "Jules, I am suffocating," she was just saying. And again: "Where is Navailles?"[9]

I beseech you, my God, hold me accountable for her sins. For they are truly mine.

Had our marriage been what it should have been, an education, an initiation, she would have remained what she was, in accord with her happy, lofty nature.

I was gravely wrong to leave her alone. I distrusted her, I disdained her. Neglected, forgotten, she doubted God. Her heart, however, remained Christian.

Since she was thus deprived of what gave her strength, dessicated and sterile, I abandoned her to the emptiness of her mind. She then assumed the failings of solitary people, of the abandoned. Of all her failings, she seemed to have chosen the one that did not harm me at all personally. Alas! It led her to her death.[10]

She did not give up so long as she could contribute to her children's education. As she found herself less useful to them, she grew despondent and, increasingly, sought oblivion.

She loved me infinitely. She wanted the infinite, or nothing. My least expression of concern for others distanced and irritated her. Alas! I find that I have lost the infinite in her, such as it exists in a human heart. At bottom, that is the only sin for which I seek forgiveness for her. What ill she did, she did because of her excessive and irrational attachment, or due to the despair of seeing that I responded to it so little.

What an unnatural and harsh thing art or knowledge is, for us thus

---

9 Pauline's half-brother. See chap. 1, n. 38.

10 Michelet alludes here to Pauline's alcoholism, her overindulgence in wine. He forgets to blame tuberculosis for her death as well.

to abandon those we truly love so much! I would leave her alone for many long Sundays, while all other families went off together to seek common pleasures... Alas! Everything I have accomplished was at the expense of her happiness and her life. If I gained any renown, it would be at her expense. Now I am bitterly repaid on the day of her death.[11]

Alas! Why must she be separated from her son? If she had to, she might have agreed to leave everything, but her son, her son! Such a separation is completely unnatural... He left her without understanding, and coldly, more astonished than touched. It broke my heart. I did not blame the child. But I wept for human nature.

I who teach the immortality of the soul, I would now give anything to believe in it with all my heart! I believe in it on a rational level. Immortality, or rather, such as we conceive of it today, immortality through migration from planet to planet,[12] or through education in this world, what can it be, after all, if you neither retain the memory of what you were or the perception of what you leave nor remember the tears of those you leave here below?

Her death weighs heavily upon me. Perhaps I could have changed her poor soul, had I seriously applied myself to doing so. What did she become, that unfortunate part of myself, while the other part wandered about in knowledge and passion? I had reduced that pitiful me who dies today to being my *sensual self*. Had I kept her in contact with my entire soul, she would have been happy, she would have lived...

---

11 Compare with Michelet's observation, in the *Memorial*, that he gained freedom at the price of his mother's life. His own son will imitate his defensive apathy.

12 Michelet alludes to his friend Jean Reynaud's articles, *Ciel* [Sky] and *Terre* [Earth], published in the *Encyclopédie nouvelle* in 1836 and 1837, respectively. The philosopher Reynaud (1806–63) was a Saint-Simonian socialist who defended the doctrine of metempsychosis, the transmigration of souls from one life form to another. Michelet will return to the *Encyclopédie* and read other articles (*Animal, Cétacés*) to find a scientific alternative to Christian dogma during Mme Dumesnil's demise; see below, entry of 30 May 1842.

Yet, it must be said, it would not have been easy to do. Daughter of such a mother, so little cared for in her childhood, then the convent school, etc. Yet, in her good moments, she had retained from all of this a *charming originality*, the vivacity of ancient France which would have raised her, as ignorant and unformed as she was, to the highest level of society... She was distinctly a *Frenchwoman*, a lively and independent personality. And with all that, she was faithful. In several respects how much worthier she was than I!

She held out during my years of hard work (until 1834). In recent years she yielded, she gave up on herself. Alas! During those years, I indulged myself excessively in the useless meanderings of imagination that estranged me from her... I return today to the home that I neglected, and I find it shattered forever...

25 July 1839, Thursday

The last lines were written an hour after her death. I remained alone in her room. My aunt[13] and my daughter were in the adjoining one. I tried to read the Psalms. But in any reading there is something too general for so individual, so intimate a grief...

At five o'clock, M. Vannestier arrived and placed the crucifix at her feet and, in front, the holy water, the candles... My daughter couldn't take it. She fled with her aunt. I sent them back to Paris.

I remained with this good and worthy man, who nonetheless bothered me a lot. His shopkeeper's gossipy vulgarity, his coarseness—superficial, I well know—wounded me constantly. He told me how he had buried his wife, his children, how their coffins were too narrow, how they hastened to place the arms closer together. Otherwise, it would have gone badly. They had to break the bones in order to force them closer, etc. While he matter-of-factly recounted all this, a hurdy-

13 Sister of Michelet's father, Mme Vannestier, who came with her husband from Rueil to care for Michelet's children and manage his household. They were simple people of modest means, true representatives of Michelet's plebeian origins.

gurdy played outside and the lady from the ground floor ruthlessly struck her piano keys.

Noon. I return to the very moment of *death*. I had her propped up. At that very moment, she threw herself sideways on her pillow and began breathing with great difficulty. Several times, there were long pauses that terrified me; I would quickly hold a bottle of smelling salts near her. But the breathing pauses became more frequent. Finally, the salts no longer helped. In my distress, I sent for Mme Cochelet's doctor, who, they said, was at her house. The chambermaid came up, casually entered the room, and asked me some stupid question. Finally, the doctor arrived and heavily placed his fat paw on her heart. —"Oh! Monsieur, gently!" The imbecile answered proudly, "Monsieur, we are doctors to do good and not ill."

She had remained with her eyes extinguished, her mouth half-open, like a miserable carp without water. There was no resounding last sigh. No grimace. Only I noticed a slight wrinkling of the nose which, little by little, disappeared.

While she was still breathing, I quickly sent my father and my son away. She had kissed him but scarcely recognized him. Although I had placed him to write in front of the window, opposite her, she no longer saw him...

I quickly wrote to Papa to ask Poret, Dargaud, Ravaisson[14] to find an artist to sketch her. The next day at eight o'clock, a young artist from Paray arrived,[15] son of a carpenter, full of feeling, good plebeian stock, who had started his career late, in spite of his parents, despite all

14 Félix Ravaisson (1813–1900) was one of Michelet's secretaries (or research assistants) between 1830 and 1838. He became an important philosopher and exercised a decisive influence on Henri Bergson.

15 Michelet begins his custom of postmortem portraits. The unnamed "young artist" was probably Tony Toullion, born in Paray-le-Monial (in the Seine et Loire department), who studied with the maréchal de Retz and Amaury-Duval. He did portraits of Michelet, Quinet, and Adam Mickiewicz around 1843, during their triumph at the Collège de France.

the obstacles, and who received as encouragement only the rigors of Amaury-Duval and his other teachers. He brought me Dargaud's excellent letter. During the day I received very touching letters from princesses.[16]

I advised the young man to close all the shutters and to draw by candlelight. The result was prodigious. Her features became more noble than they had ever been while she was alive. She was yellow, but noble and without wrinkles. She stood out marvelously against the red scarf and the white pillow. I had put the scarf and white bonnet on her only a few hours before her death.

Strange day, and of eternal memory. Freed from M. Vannestier, who was running errands, I passed the time looking at my treasure, who still remained in my care for a day, or else I spoke about her to the young painter. I tried to make him enter into the character of the person he was painting but whom he had not known. I made him notice that absence of wrinkles on her forehead, that perfect simplicity she had retained on her face and in her heart.

I believe that I kindled the young man's heart. With words or with pencil we incubated that death and quickened it with our vitality.

M. Aupépin came around four o'clock and wept. That opened my heart to him again. He made the incision in her arm, as I had requested.[17] A deep incision, to the bone, which opened two white lips in the flesh. But no more blood...

Dargaud arrived at seven o'clock and stayed until eleven. The young man stayed and left only when Dargaud did. He had sketched for fourteen hours. His last sketch is truly tragic. It expresses the dismal atmosphere of that evening, of that sepulchral room, of that poor face that can no longer breathe.

---

16 Michelet tutored the daughters of the Orléans family: Clémentine, Louise, and Marie. Louis-Philippe had eight children.

17 Like many of his contemporaries, Michelet was obsessed with the possibility of a premature burial.

M. Vannestier returned, excited, and *almost jolly*. I harshly felt this contrast. He wanted to eat more *supper*. I had lots of water put in his wine.

He had watched the body the first night, with the doorkeeper. The second night, she did the night vigil with our maid, Madeleine. M. V... would sleep only on the couch, where he snored until morning.

26 July 1839, Friday

The horrible ordeal of the burial finally took place... With the help of the doorkeeper and Madeleine, we succeeded in putting on her bonnet (her most beautiful one), scarf, and white blouse. We removed, by cutting it, the poor little flannel vest, which she had taken off for me and which I put on her in the final days.

Alas! The odor was already strong, her belly greenish, her nose blackened. I horribly felt, and to the marrow, the words of Job: "I said to the worms: You are my brothers; I said to decay: You are my sister."[18] It is awful to feel oneself detached. The first day, my children had felt horror and fear. As for me, I continued *until the third*. Alas! Nature, the senses began to weaken. Disgust came (must I admit it?) for the pitiful remains that had been a desired, adored woman, for that lovable form who, for twenty years, had renewed my insatiable passion...

I had sent for a cross of everlasting flowers[19] to place on her body, under her shroud. They could only find one wreath. I set it down and, on her shroud, I placed a crucifix.

Her face remained uncovered. I kissed it, already cold and ashen, several times... Finally, I had to tear myself away. The coffin was in the room, the bearers were waiting. —"Farewell, farewell Pauline." I still did not leave. I myself tried to tie the shroud above her head,

18 Book of Job 17: 14 (from the Service for the Dead, 7th lesson).

19 In French, *immortelles*, colorful dried flowers.

but I was unable. I watched her being placed in the coffin, and I threw holy water on her with tremendous heartbreak.

However, these struggles were somewhat beneficial: I realized that the flesh that dissolved in my hands could no longer be *herself*. That idea thrust me back into spiritualism, into faith in *the beyond*. Had I left her in her true and whole form, it would have been like leaving a living person. By dint of waiting and watching, I became convinced that I left only a thing... The person is no longer here. Let us hope that she is elsewhere...

Only friends joined the funeral procession, those who truly mourned her. MM. Dargaud, Aupépin, Millet,[20] Poret, Vannestier. That was better than a crowd. However, the solitude saddened me. I thought that I should have honored her differently, by allowing her to share, as much as I could, the esteem that many people have for me...

What a revelation death is! It unveils at one blow the good that was hidden in mankind...

30 July 1839, Tuesday

Oh, how I need to embrace the homeland, increasingly to know and to love France! I had, so close to me, a living and true representative of the French spirit, a naïve French individual: I lost her...

I have said it elsewhere: *France is a person*.[21] True personality, therefore, very much *one;* nevertheless, quite complex. What is that unity? France is the country of grace, of harmonized movement, of reconciled conflicts.

–Michelet elucidated his complex reactions to Pauline's death. Writing the *Journal* helped him to analyze his bereavement; aware of

20 Michelet's cousin, Xavier-Félix Millet, a notary in the town of Provins, was the son of the brother of the historian's mother.

21 *Introduction to Universal History* (1831).

his past self-deception, he bravely attempted to distinguish truth from pious wishes. But he did not always succeed. The entries of July 1839 suggest that the survivor nurtured his pain, in large part, to divert his attention from appropriate reasons for guilt. Grief punished his selfishness, but, instead of taking full responsibility, he blamed spiritual strivings for the failings of his will: "What an unnatural and harsh thing art or knowledge is, for us thus to abandon those we truly love so much!" His most serious mistake was to believe that a conflict between love and work was irremediable.

The historian chronicled the minute details of Pauline's decline, studied his "anticipatory grief," in order, progressively, to brace himself for the definitive loss. He attempted to love her according to his ideal of marriage, but his ambivalence prevailed. Through an ironic act of psychological justice, his long, woeful walks to the clinic needled his conscience. The poignant sweetness of their enhanced communication seemed to be advance retribution for his abusive self-concern: "our hearts drew closer [. . .] probably to make the separation sadder, to increase the heartbreak." Michelet censured himself indirectly as he deplored the apparent coldness of their ten-year-old Charles.

To tame his moral conflict, the widower split himself into at least two selves. True, he had lost part of himself to death. But he confessed that he had used Pauline to relieve his tensions; she had become his "sensual self," an instrument of his "individual self." What a delusion to regret that he did not absorb her into his "entire soul"! He humbled himself while maintaining the grandiose notion that he could have saved her. The survivor then summoned his "literary self" and his "moral self" to redeem Pauline's noble traits. The day before the funeral, on 25 July, the *Journal* deliberately returned "to the very moment of *death*." A gruesome description of her final moments highlights his own anguished—and perhaps inappropriate—attempts to postpone her decease by uncomfortably propping her up in bed. To possess her entirely, he dismissed his father and son and sent for an artist who would capture the essence of Pauline's personality unveiled by death. The historian thus established another ritual: He hired a painter to reinforce his literary resurrection.

Michelet never separated art and life. He tacitly identified with the young plebeian painter and, with him, achieved esthetic distance, that delicate combination of objectivity and passion from which art is born. As he had done at Poinsot's exhumation, Michelet imagined that he revived the corpse: "With words or with pencil we incubated that death and quickened it with our vitality." Their powers seemed magical, but only Michelet's artistic self remained confident. The philosopher, or "moral self," skeptically questioned his faith, as he quickly admitted that he "would now give anything to believe in [immortality] with all [his] heart." Part of him neutralized her extinction while his other part could not deny it. Another struggle for inner harmony.

The widower postponed the crisis by incorporating his confused thoughts into his philosophy of history. His fascination with Pauline's corpse betrayed the competition within his mind between materialism and poetic vision. The day of the funeral, 26 July, he stared at her decay and began to accept her death, but only for a moment: "I realized that the flesh that dissolved in my hands could no longer be *herself*. [. . .] The person is no longer here. Let us hope that she is elsewhere." On 30 July a provisional solution emerged. If he could not wholeheartedly believe that the individual soul survived, he could reaffirm the guiding image of France as a person. His collective human entity guaranteed mankind's unbreachable continuity across the vicissitudes of time. Pauline, whom the historian had just surrendered, would thus endure within the collective body. He transformed her into a symbol of the motherland, "a living and true representative of the French spirit." The poet transcended personal loss as he envisioned "reconciled conflicts."

ANNIVERSARY MOURNING

The survivor's conscience, his "moral self," continued to goad. On 22 August 1839, Michelet will anticipate the one-month anniversary of his wife's death with an impatient review of his bereavement. His prose will reach great poetic heights as he evokes "death's tender graces." The widower had become more receptive to nuances, as it were, "tinted with the universal color of grief," and he begins to separate his tremendous ego from the true expressions of love he perceived in his dying wife's eyes. But even the quest for self-knowledge cannot explain why he so militantly "preserved this grief." Why did he treasure sorrow above all? The following entry suggests that he was preparing to die.

Michelet's poetry of bereavement played out one irreducible contradiction. He attempted to dominate his own fear of dying by plunging into his grief, savoring the horror of rotting flesh, and caressing the deceased. At one and the same time, the writer revered death and denied its finality, as he sought to formulate a theory of immortality that would clarify death's still enigmatic charm.

22 August 1839, Thursday

One month after Pauline's death. *Individuality, personality*. We were speaking about the daguerreotype. What does it need to become a painting of the great masters? It needs a lot... And what is missing? Their flaws. But their flaws are nothing other than themselves, than their personalities. Our perfect side is our general dimension, it is less ourselves. Our bad side is unquestionably ours. That is what is unfair about loving the individual side: It is because we love also, even especially love, the flaws.

Yes, I loved her for her flaws. First, one loves everything about the loved one. Then, unfortunately, her flaws were mine; at least, they came to her from me. Perhaps that is why we separated. I loved in her the bad I had put there. It is a cruel fact that I had given flaws to her that I myself did not have, because my natural brutality was counterbalanced in me by the driving force of ideas.

Alas! Must I believe that that poor soul bears the weight with which I burdened her, that she now departs, weighed down with this muddy clay, burdened with a fatality that comes from me, whom she loved so much? Does she remember me? If so, then perhaps she hates me. But that cannot be. And if she does not remember, she has probably lost all memory of this life. Then she suffers without knowing why.

Perhaps one must believe, with Spinoza,[22] that those in whom ideas lose their vitality will die completely, little by little. And I don't know if I would prefer that for her, terrified as I am of future punishments. Moreover, if the punishments are proportionate to the responsibility, hers is light, mine great. Practically everything she willed was through me.

For two days my dog has been anxious and sad. He whines, he searches. Perhaps, at long last, he is afflicted because he no longer sees her return...

May I preserve this grief! I will not trade it for all the joys. Having tasted death so perfectly is a great preparation for someone who will also die. Having seen her, so to speak, melt and disappear in my hands, that pitiful flesh of my flesh that I had so often kissed, is also to be dead oneself.

Alas! To feel repugnance for what was as much me as the self who survives, that is a cruel divorce...

And the moment, the final half-hour, when her breathing stopped at intervals until I brought the salts and revived her and made her renew her ties with life, that too is a painful and pitiable memory. There I saw, through my tears, death's tender graces which I did not suspect, tender, but so doleful that I remained shattered to the depths of my existence...

She had never been able to witness suffering: A carp out of water would pain her. Oh! May her kindness be credited to her, to soothe the cruel moment when her heart lacked air.

But an even more disturbing memory is the next-to-the-last morning, from four to eight o'clock, so tender and so painful. I then discovered everything that love and sorrow contain. What could life teach me now? She no longer spoke and expressed herself only through the

---

22 Michelet considered the Dutch philosopher Baruch Spinoza (1632–77) to represent a materialistic and pantheistic philosophy in which the individual soul was absorbed into the All.

feeble cries of a suffering child. This childhood at the supreme moment is something deeply moving and disturbing... What could she have been thinking? Probably regret at leaving us. She was visibly sad, but without tears. Her large eyes, her long looks, penetrated my heart; her love too. Alas! I could not give her my life in return.

"My grief," said the father of Amy Robsart, abducted by Leicester (Walter Scott), "is like this castle where you see me: the paths which surround it all converge there, all lead there..."[23]

There is much more. The more the mind is cultivated, the more aspects and facets there are, the more are exterior objects reflected in it, tinted with the universal color of grief. My grief is like smallpox: It is only after the attack that the effects deepen and make scars.

–Although he claimed to have loved Pauline's flaws as well as her virtues, his guilty self longed for her eternal soul to forgive him. His basic moral conflict came to this: Had the husband's "natural brutality [been] counterbalanced [. . .] by the driving force of [his] ideas?" Could his goals justify his rigid work habits? Unfortunately, Michelet's oversimplification of the problem—separating his good and bad, spiritual and physical selves—made it impossible to resolve the conflict. He did not apply the truism that all mortals are imperfect, a mixture of lofty and base motives, to himself. As Kierkegaard might have said, the widower lacked the purity of heart to will one thing.

As he had done in 1821 at Poinsot's death, Michelet sketched a biography of the departed. On the one-month anniversary of his wife's demise, he would seek to restore the past. With their children, he visited the village of Meaux, where Pauline had gone to convent school. He dined with the bishop of Meaux, Monseigneur Auguste Allou (1793–1885), a former companion at the Collège Charlemagne, and conversed with the Scellier women, the mother and two daughters who had befriended Pauline during her lonely school years. Two places organized his quest: (1) the bishop's home, which recalled

[23] Michelet refers to the play by Victor Hugo, *Amy Robsart* (1828), inspired by Walter Scott.

seventeenth-century religious controversies between Bossuet,[24] the Jesuit orator of Louis XIV's court, and the mystical author Fénelon,[25] whose *Spiritual Letters* the bereaved historian read for consolation; and (2) the convent that witnessed Pauline's youth. Michelet will combine technical historical research and introspection.

24 August 1839, Saturday

Went by carriage. Excessively small cathedral bearing upon the steps like Sainte-Gudule of Brussels. Nudity of the church, beautiful in its nobility and lightness, unornamented. Bad statue of Bossuet. The Gobelins borrowed their precious collection of paintings inspired by the Raphael designs, more complete than the Hampton Court collection. Episcopal palace; staircase without steps, twelfth-century chapel, ultramodern drawing room that the present bishop believes he must justify.

Some of the gardens on the city ramparts. Bossuet's office, which had been ruined under Bonaparte, has been restored, with the room of the servant who used to wake him in the morning. The path of yew trees, planted by Bossuet's predecessor. One of the beauties of these terraces and of this garden is that above, from every side, one can see the imposing tower of the cathedral. The dark path, under fifteenth-century archways, leads to this noble garden, shadeless like the great orator's soul. Then one notices that this garden also has its shadows; the office is coldly bare. The yew path is quite dark. *Quid*, whether this excessively external life finally found there its inwardness? The

---

24 Jacques-Bénigne Bossuet (1627–1704), named in 1681 bishop of Meaux, wrote magnificent sermons, funeral orations, and polemics. He was the leading churchman of the court: tutor to Louis, duc de Bourgogne, the dauphin, eldest son of Louis de France, the only son of Louis XIV and Marie-Thérèse. He vigorously attacked quietism, a mystical movement represented by the archbishop of Cambrai, Fénelon.

25 François de Salignac de La Mothe-Fénelon (1651–1715) started as a disciple of Bossuet and became the spiritual leader of a devout group at the court. He was named archbishop of Cambrai in 1695 but came into conflict with the king and Bossuet when he defended the quietist mystic Mme Guyon. Michelet wrote fervent pages about these debates in *About Priests, Women, and the Family,* published in 1845.

bishop, an old friend, M. Allou, moved me as he explained how he was going to settle there and how there had been no reluctance, when...

I, who have been *settled* and who, despite my children, am scarcely settled today, I was making this serious voyage to Bossuet, whose palace I was visiting, Fénelon, whose *Spiritual Letters* I was reading, and a completely different memory of which I find here so few traces,[26] perhaps not even in her best friend!...

I learned that the nun (from the Enfant Jésus order) who had accompanied her here in 1814, and who may still be here, was named Mlle Martin (Sister des Anges).

Yesterday, as I was crossing this beautiful countryside gilded by autumn and the evening sun, as I saw that land bursting with nature's gifts, I found it quite hard to accept that so little of her remained there... What! Only six feet of earth? I dare not add all my thoughts; they are irrational. In our materialistic habits of thought, we pity the body as though it were the person. Probably the soul is not within that sad coffin... But it is nonetheless cruel for survivors to be able to do nothing for her other than pray, —probably not very useful prayers.

Nightfall overtook us on the road. The moon was triumphantly bright. Nature's indifference increases the heartache...[27] In the evening, I read from Fénelon (letter 104): "The dying Saint Ambrose was asked whether he was not afflicted by the fear of God's judgments. He answered: We have a good master." Oh! Never have I more vividly felt the need to believe in that kindness.

25 August 1839, Sunday

Today, magnificent weather, but it gives me a headache. First I went

26 The widower finally recalls Pauline.

27 Michelet anticipates the important poem of Alfred de Vigny (1797–1863), "La Maison du berger," first published in the *Revue des deux mondes* in 1844. The Romantic poet depicts Nature as an insensitive witness to human suffering.

alone to visit the beautiful cathedral and the odd castle with four turrets next to it. Then His Grace, the bishop, at nine. At high mass, very few people and only women. Mlles Scellier at noon. Lunch. Then their little garden, sad and hot. Then I read and slept. Now (six o'clock in the evening) I am writing while they dine at their godmother's house. Wonderful letters of Fénelon (110, 111) on his suffering: "But all is well... God opens a strange book for our benefit..." And again: "I am, unto myself, a large complete diocese..."

This evening, after dinner and tea, walked alone under Bossuet's terrace; outside, far-off noise of military music. The cathedral at sunset created a wonderful harmony. Then I entered the episcopal palace, walking with about twenty priests. They complained about M. Villemain,[28] who refuses the certificates from small seminaries for baccalaureate admissions... Concerning the noble quarrel between Bossuet and Fénelon, His Grace said: "Fortunately, those disputes are over." —Fortunately? He wants me to omit: "A virtue has emerged from me."

26 August 1839, Monday

Coffee at Mlle Scellier's house. Then, while waiting for the hospital's visiting hours, walked with Mlle Adélaïde Scellier along the hospital walls, the Marne River, and the market of Meaux. Toured the hospital guided by Mme Scellier and a young nun of Saint-Vincent-de-Paul, born, she said, in 1815, the very year my wife entered the hospital. Visited the huge garden, where she had walked so many times with Mlle Scellier, the lilacs that Mlle Scellier planted with her! the fruit trees, etc. We could not see the rooms that the nuns then occupied. That section is uninhabited. But we saw the room that serves both as

[28] We recall that A.-F. Villemain had been Michelet's faithful support since his student days at the Collège Charlemagne. Villemain had recently become minister of education (a post he held until 1844) and opposed attempts by the Jesuits to have religious schools validated by the state.

school and as refectory for the girls, the chair between the two windows... I did not dare express any of my thoughts in the presence of this old lady Scellier, so detached from affectionate bonds for so long. But I noticed, seeing all the poor come to her, that her true family was here. These poor people seem jolly... But they no longer have the same gentleness, nor did the nun. No more cows, no more chickens, nothing from that little convent household that had amused my wife and Mlle Scellier. Today's nuns can offer only nice words, or a caress to the dying, as I saw at the infirmary. I wish I could give a large donation to that poor establishment, which at one time sheltered the one who had since shared my poverty for twenty years...

We must learn to die. After a life of individuality, we must begin one of generality, if possible. But how can we bury, without a tear, such a precious part of our heart? How many wasted happy days, uselessly passed together, now forever impossible! But can we ever experience anything happy in our individuality? Did any day of our union, which we missed so much, ever pass entirely without storm? "Come now, noble doctor, hold fast," as Luther said at the death of his daughter, Magdalen.

Lunch at the bishop's, a good, simple, likable, average man. However, he seemed to elevate himself a bit by his feeling for art. Everywhere in the church he had the small, lower pointed arches removed. Bossuet's tombstone was placed behind the choir, the body remained among those of the bishops, but we don't know precisely where. M. de Bissy effected that fine operation. I saw at the bishop's house a beautiful bust of Cardinal Polignac, the *Anti-Lucretius*,[29] and the painting of one of the latest bishops, also of the Polignac family. Beautiful contrast: large, scheming and bold face; the other quite pretty. In the salon itself, in the bishop's house, Salamander in front

29 Cardinal Melchior de Polignac (1661–1742) was a writer and political figure whose Latin poem, *Anti-Lucretius*, sought to refute materialism.

of the hearth (Briçonnet, bishop). In Bossuet's office, over the hearth, lovely full-length portrait of the princess. The huge pearl she wore in her belt reminded me of the pearl or diamond that the dying Madame placed on Bossuet's finger; could this be she?[30]

I returned by the mailboat. Immobility greater than in a stagecoach. Overcome by this rapid sequence of objects, without much variety, however, which run by above us, whereas in a carriage you have a gratifying sense of floating above. Two seminarians from Meaux were seated opposite us, quite pedantic and quite surly. They spoke about me and my books with little charity... My first impulse was to say: "So that is the controversial reputation to which I have sacrificed my family's happiness." But upon reflection I took heart. This is not the testimony that the future will bestow upon a sincere writer. Even priests are generally more sympathetic to me. What does it matter, after all! I love them more than they love me. He who loves most comes out ahead.

* * *

THE CRISIS OF PAULINE'S EXHUMATION

–Michelet will complete his farewell when he has Pauline's corpse moved to another gravesite the week after his visit to Meaux.[31] She had been buried for just over a month, and he should not have been surprised that her flesh was still crawling with maggots and worms. His horror was somewhat mixed with pleasure, however, as he interpreted his discomfort moralistically: "penance, both for the pride of beauty and for the temptation of desire." Simultaneously, he remembered his delights while he reviled his selfishness. Michelet will also realize, and finally admit in his *Journal*, that, almost consciously, he

---

[30] *Madame* was the duchesse d'Orléans, wife of *Monsieur*, King Louis XIV's eldest brother.

[31] Bishop Allou had Bossuet's body exhumed in November 1854. The old friends had more in common than the historian at first realized.

wanted to die and annihilate his own body. He dwelt upon the esthetics of death with such grim determination in order, indirectly, to work out his own suicidal impulses.

4 September 1839, Wednesday

Exhumation: 8:00 a.m. Stormy morning, after the rain.

Severe ordeal. Alas! I scarcely saw anything but worms. It is said: "returned to the earth." It is a figure of speech. The corpse's inanimate substance reanimates a living substance. That aspect is hideous to the eye, harsh as Christian humiliation, great, cruelly poetic and philosophical for the mind. What a penance, both for the pride of beauty and for the temptation of desire!

That I, who came with my heart full of her, overwhelmed with pity and love, eager to see her features again, for at least a minute, should not have been able to endure the sight! I who still, around 1 June (she left the sixth for Passy)...

The body's shape was better preserved under the shroud; greenish, but already harshly projecting or heavily round, like something that collapses...

This cemetery, amidst the roses and the honeysuckle, seems like a paradise. What terrible ugliness beneath! However, when I observed the gaping grave from above, I powerfully felt, as I have felt on the sea or from the top of a tower, the attraction of death! *O mihi tum quam molliter ossa quiescant!* [Oh, may my bones then rest sweetly!][32] However, I placed a token there: some of my hair in a sheet of her

---

32 Virgil, *Bucolics*, book 10, line 33. Michelet first cited this verse in his *Journal* entry of 4 August 1820. The context was quite significant. The young man considered sexual relations with women as a tragic reminder of a man's mortality: " 'A rubbing of the penis, a little convulsion, an ejection of semen,' said Marcus-Aurelius. That act through which your mad passion will soften you, weaken you, will not give you what you seek. [. . .] With despair you will bite the adored body with which you cannot be one. That powerlessness causes the melancholy of love, and thoughts of death that are constantly mixed with love: ...*O mihi tum quam molliter ossa quiescant!*"

son's writing; in addition, a metal cross, waiting for the moment I join her altogether...

But I must not let myself go. What would become of our children? She herself was so afraid of "leaving her daughter alone."

Farewell. I must abstain even from writing about this sad and too alluring subject. In order to obey her, I must force myself to subdue even my regrets, to think of them less, in order to live and continue her thought, her providential care over what she leaves behind.

Poor soul... For her I pledge myself to two tasks that should ease her ordeals, wherever she may be. First, she was preoccupied with the lofty thought of preserving her daughter's purity. Then, she had assumed gentle and benevolent feelings for the person of whom she was jealous; obviously, she did not hate him any more.[33]

* * *

12 September 1839, Thursday

Saint-Cloud. Each life has its ripe age, its yellowing season. May the heavens grant that this be my ripe age! But it is not advanced age. It is the age when hope diminishes, when effort is certainly useless, when a wall rises up and stops you short. Moreover, when you arrive there, you cannot pass beyond; you have done what you had to do. There are not, as is believed, many abridged destinies. Death is then, as Fénelon said in another context, "a remedy for the deep affliction of our nature."

Another generation must therefore begin everything anew at its own expense.

How to make people believe this, and to believe it oneself, that the extinction of the personality is a benefit? Alas! each man is a complete universal history, a world. That false little universality confronts the grand and devouring universality of the all...

I experienced a deep sadness one day when, on the seashore, at Le Havre, I saw my little daughter (six years old) throwing rocks at

---

33 Pauline had become violently resentful of Furcy Michelet's supervision of her husband's life and household.

the sea: The sea threw waves at her. That unequal struggle between the finite and the infinite, whose result is so inevitable, wrung tears from me.[34]

The person, a specific person: a unique thing; nothing similar, nothing after... May other generations come, better in every sense. Ah! It will not be the same, it will not be this individual, transient person. And yet, she possessed ideas about the future, about immortality. What! Such a small container, such vast contents...

One person, how many unnoticed threads entangled her with other personalities! Examine, trace them closer and closer, you will shudder. One notices all the threads at the time of death, because they break or are laid bare. Like the threads and the creeping vines of ivy that I noticed yesterday in the forest of Saint-Germain: I ripped off the leaves, but the vines had gripped the bark so well that I had to separate them with iron.

The death of a person is a terrible upheaval for the mind! We recall so many things! How much we examine what we meant to her! At that moment judgment begins for us, and inner accusation. We judge her for each moment, and with bitterness. We judge her on the totality, on her entire life. Thus considered, she gains so much! Oh! May God so judge her. *Oh time, beautifier of things!*[35] But neither time nor death lies about this. Rather, life was the liar. It exaggerated the bad.

Why are thoughts of God such meager consolation? Because the Christian God will judge her soul. She will live on: but to suffer? The God of pantheism will give her rest, but by absorbing her...

---

[34] Michelet recalls his *Journal* entry of 6 August 1831, which described his daughter throwing pebbles at the waves: "As I saw, on one side that horrifying image of the infinite, on the other my daughter, and that attraction which calls us back to nature's abyss, I felt the fabric of individual existence sunder. The homeland of mankind is the general, the universal, the eternal." Michelet returned to this symbolic event in *The Sea* (1861).

[35] Michelet quotes in English from Byron, *Childe Harold's Pilgrimage* (canto 4, line 130), quoted also in the course of 1839, lesson 17 of 24 June.

Why do we so often miss our depraved friends more than the others?

1. Because we ourselves are depraved, and we mourn them in our own nature. 2. We often believe ourselves to be the partial cause of their vices. 3. We are more anxious about their future destiny.

Yet we present so many excuses to God, as we believe that evil results, most often, from external influences.

As for me, I have many excuses for so many things, regrets for so many different eras. I, for whom each past life is precious and who feel all humanity as part of my family and my blood, I stride through history bearing this great urn, like the Greek actor who, playing Electra, carried the urn of his own son...

How death enlightens! How it tears words from the heart! "Let us pretend to be brave as much as we can... *Eriptur persona, manet res.* [The mask is torn away, the thing remains.]" Death is charity's boundless helper; it teaches us the great truth that in each man there is more good than evil.

We believe; *we believe that we believe.* But if the blow strikes close to us, we become materialists. Says Satan in Job: "Yes, but touch his skin, you will see..."[36] Then we are humbled. Luther said: "I cannot really believe that Saint Paul had believed as strongly as he said."

I have seen the proudest spiritualist, when his skin was touched, as Satan said, irresistibly drawn by the powerful attractions of the grave, follow it like a dog, pursue with a painful hunger the tomb's horrifying ugliness, and without satisfying his need, repeating the dismal story of Inès de Castro.[37]

---

36 Book of Job 1:11.

37 Michelet alludes to the "dismal story of Inès de Castro" in volume 5 of the *History of France* (book 6, chap. 1), on the reign of Charles V, that will appear in August 1841. Inès de Castro (1310–55) was the secret mistress and wife of Dom Pedro of Portugal; she was murdered by his father, King Alfonso IV. When Pedro became king he killed the assassins and exhumed his wife, crowned her rotted corpse, and

Ah! We must agree that these are not idle words: "You become the same flesh." Communion of home, of bread, of bed, of children. Great God! What more? Fed by man's work, she ate his sweat and, still more directly, she received him into her womb. And, having received him thus in her womb, she then carried him for nine months, so becoming his mother, after having been his wife. Strange and peculiar mystery.

To live one for the other, man bringing sustenance and woman giving it to him, as the mother bird feeds from her beak. Every day confiding his ideas to her, finding in one another such a sweet forgetfulness of self, each evening dying within each other, dying and creating together, being gods together!

She, in whom each evening you found self-forgetfulness and that intoxicating death of self called love. For me she was nature in its lively spontaneity, devoted to my individuality, beyond nature, against nature...

Everything together, then nothing together: It is dying more than if we both had died...

14 September 1839, Saturday

Even though I was sick twice, and felt a severe nervous weakness, I worked at the Institut. Dr. Edwards[38] convinced me to take a trip, Burnouf[39] and Mme Angelet[40] confirmed his judgment. So let us see

---

forced the courtesans to kiss her bony hand. Michelet's obsession also passed into the *History of the French Revolution* (book 8, chap. 8), as he depicts Danton exhuming his wife one week after her death: "he fought the worms for her, horrible and disfigured, with a frantic embrace"; see also book 11, chap. 4.

38 William Frederic Edwards (1777–1842), born in Jamaica of English parents, studied in France and became a brilliant physiologist; he wrote on linguistics, physics, and physiology. Michelet and Edwards became friends in May 1829 after Michelet read his *Letter to Thierry* on races.

39 We recall Michelet's dream of June 1837 in which Eugène Burnouf appears. Burnouf was elected to the Académie des inscriptions et belles-lettres in 1832 when Champollion, the translator of the Rosetta stone, died in the cholera epidemic. Burnouf guided Michelet's reading of Hindu literature.

if I will regain a bit of my electricity, which seems to have been completely drained during these recent crises.

18 September 1839, Wednesday

I painfully separated myself from our sad house, from her portrait. At 7:00 a.m. I left on the Royal coach service which, at 7:00 p.m., brought us to Dieppe. [. . .]

MOTHER DEATH UNVEILED

–The inspired entry of 12 September confronted the three fundamental causes of the author's grief: (1) his contrition for having debased Pauline; (2) his struggle to replace philosophical uncertainty with religious faith; and (3) his uncanny attraction to death. Pauline's sickness and death had stripped his defenses, advanced his self-knowledge, and yet guilt maintained its despotism. Not only did Michelet confess that he sacrificed his wife to ambition; he tacitly admitted responsibility for his humiliating refusals to share nights with her. Only at the very end of the 4 September entry, almost as an afterthought, did the widower defensively claim that his dying wife had ceased hating his father. At the same time, death allowed Michelet a convenient victory, for he continued to share his father's bedroom until Furcy died seven years later.

Michelet sensitively disclosed the reasons for his guilt but rarely interpreted them accurately, until now. The exhumation of 4 September enabled him ritually to atone for all sins. He violated Pauline's repose and threw into the pit tokens of his own self-sacrifice: a lock of his hair wrapped in his son's writing and a metal cross. He surrendered these fetishes of himself to the earth in order to anticipate, and perhaps to stave off, "the moment I join her altogether." But he

40 Mme Angelet was the governess of Princess Clémentine, Louis-Philippe's daughter, whom Michelet began to tutor after the July (1830) Revolution. When Michelet traveled he wrote long, detailed letters to the princess through Mme Angelet, most of which, unfortunately, have been lost. The historian resigned as tutor on 24 June 1845.

soon recognized those impulses as pathological and rebelled against them. He himself was the "proud spiritualist" driven to repeat "the dismal story of Inès de Castro," whose husband Pedro I of Portugal publicly exhumed her three years after burial.

Michelet contemplated his wife's putrescence to convince himself that the person was mortal and that her soul would endure. Anguished, he wavered between the wish for individual immortality (his "proud spiritualism") and the gross evidence of finitude. His writing pulsed with a subtle poetic pathos as he attempted to reconcile Pauline's destruction with his sad but hopeful vision of eternal existence. History allowed him to deny death by absorbing *individual* life into the *general*. It was a basic philosophical conflict. Did a person disappear into the cosmos or itself become a world? Michelet would have it both ways as his autobiography recapitulated that "complete universal history."

Deeper, less conscious needs also explain the historian's utter fascination with death and the abundant writings provoked by sorrow. The intricate ethical speculations of 12 September led directly to this astounding intuition: He yearned to surrender his adult personality and return to the womb! Michelet's sexual relations with Pauline had blessed him with "self-forgetfulness and that intoxicating death of self called love." Memories of his mother and Mme Fourcy must certainly have reinforced his nuptial bliss. The *Journal* elaborated a wonderful pre-Freudian fable about a grown man who nourished his wife, and then himself returned to a prenatal state: "She [. . .] carried him for nine months, so becoming his mother, after having been his wife. Strange and peculiar mystery." Indeed! No clearer statement of Michelet's confusion of love and death can be found. So Pauline, when alive, symbolized Mother France. After her nauseating exhumation she assumed yet another incarnation, that of Nature as destroyer.

Michelet made a trip to Normandy from 18 to 23 September that helped him regain "electricity" and soften the pain. Then he visited Versailles and again probed deeply into himself. The two remaining entries of 1839 fully absorb his bereavement into his art. In one the author lovingly will associate his inner melancholy with the brilliant and crisp fall landscape, reenacting the "pathetic fallacy" of Romantic poets who projected their emotions onto nature. The other entry will complete his responsibility for Pauline's epitaph. Accepting the autumn of his own life, his maturity, the widower returned to the house at no. 49, rue de la Roquette, where he had loved and married Pauline.[41] His historical imagination sought to resurrect the family romance: Pauline, Mme Fourcy, Poinsot, all deceased, and his living father who had silently presided.

13 October 1839, Sunday

Versailles. This beautiful season, in its maturity, makes me take stock of myself. Although still young, I lean toward my autumn...

The sight of Paris in the fog is always solemn. Touching gentleness of autumn: all of life's gifts, of life that flees... Rich and austere colors of the dahlias, of the crimson leaves. The pond of Plessis-Picquet, the path toward Aulnay, the roads to Meudon and Versailles, the Fosse-Davin, narrow passage that leads to Châtillon. Charming countryside!

The setting sun, behind us, flooded the landscape by flashes, through the yellow and purple leaves, with a pale gold of autumn.

Alas! Death deprives her of so many sweet things...

20 October 1839, Sunday

Today, Sunday, almost three months after her death, I went to see the tombstone and its almost engraved inscription.[42] Cloudy weather, already cold, but the leaves are not half fallen.

On the way, we visited M. Vial in order to see that house again, *my* house, where I was married, where my daughter was born, where I had been happy—although it was such a stormy happiness, so badly managed—where I lost so many irretrievable days because of my savage way of living, when happiness was close. That house had

---

[41] Afterward they had moved to the rue de l'Arbalète, also close to the Père-Lachaise cemetery, in April 1827.

[42] Pauline's epitaph is printed at the beginning of this chapter.

been Sedaine's.[43] When M. Vial bought it, he found there, hidden under a stone bench, the skeleton of a young woman.

My octagonal study is the same, as is the location of my poor former little bookcase and the room where I slept on the floor, on mattresses, when I spat blood in 1827 and my wife took such good care of me.[44] M. de Angelis[45] was then out to sea and, when I heard the great winds at night, I feared for him... I remember all this quite clearly.

The room where I slept with my father and the one in which Mme Fourcy died have been changed. Poinsot stayed near me in the first one, on the bed my father let him have. That bizarre night scene occurred there, when she thought I was crazy because I had gotten up to watch that uncanny spring night...

I found that M. Vial, his wife, and Mlle Julie had all aged greatly. That change in people struck me all the more in a place where everything remained young in my imagination.

My Pauline's little garden is completely buried, wet. The little shed no longer exists, nor, consequently, does the spot where we sat on the ground, one Sunday evening, after everyone had left.

Under the terrace were our kitchen and Mme de Girac's[46] bedroom, where I was ill in 1827 with my great illness after writing

---

43 Michel-Jean Sedaine (1719–97) was a dramatist, born in Paris, who began as a poor stonemason. The characters of his plays and comic operas were usually peasants and working people.

44 Michelet almost died of the pneumonia he had contracted in November 1826; the following month, barely recovered, he completed his introduction to Vico, *Principles of the Philosophy of History, Translated from Vico and Preceded by a Discourse on Vico's System and Life*, which went on sale on 8 March 1827.

45 Pietro de Angelis (1789–1860), a former secretary to King Murat, fled Italy in 1815. Victor Cousin sent M. de Angelis to Michelet to help him translate Vico's *Scienza nuova*.

46 Mme de Girac (or Mme de Girard) was one of the old ladies Pauline cared for at their new home on the rue de l'Arbalète.

Vico, when I said to Pauline: "Pauline, farewell!" Who would then have told me that I would survive?

I pray that God grant me more resignation...

* * *

A POETRY OF BEREAVEMENT (1839–1840)

–Michelet's anguish penetrated his historical re-creations. He began his first course on the Italian Renaissance on 6 January 1840. His celebration of Europe's cultural rebirth was one response to Pauline's demise, while volume 4 of the *History of France* evoked the fifteenth-century dances of death with the convulsive authenticity of effective literature. After the book appeared in February 1840, many readers, shocked by its disquieting fervor, condemned the author's "immoral inspiration."[47]

This period also heralded a renewal of love when Michelet met the mother of one of his most enthusiastic students at the Collège de France, Mme Adèle Dumesnil. The "white angel," as he would call her, made her début in the *Journal* on 24 May 1840, although they first met on 5 May. She was his age, forty-one years old, and separated from her husband. The bereaved historian valued Mme Dumesnil's intelligence and sensitivity and welcomed her into his family circle. At the same time, he continued to frequent Pauline's grave. With perseverance he pondered their shared past and transmuted his grief into poetry.

24 May 1840, Sunday

Visited cemetery with my children. Never so long an absence: the wreaths spoiled, spiders, as if the grave were possessed by solitude. During this month, however, I reflected and prayed every single day. But in the evening it seemed more worthwhile, even if I just thought about it, to look after her children, that very frail big girl. Almost every day I took them to exercise classes.

---

47 See below, entry of 29 April 1841.

During this same month, I received a letter from Mme Renart and a visit from Mme Dumesnil on behalf of her son.[48]

Right now the cemetery is a true Oriental garden, between the rose and the nightingale. In some places it is a well-kept garden, in others it seems neglected, leafy, overgrown. Delicious solitudes, where nature buries and hides the old stone under flowers.

Amidst all these beauties, one thing moved me. In the same enclosure are buried Mme de Méré, a twenty-four-year-old widow, and her five-year-old daughter. The daughter died in May, the mother in August, of the same year. The little girl has this epitaph: *At her mother's feet.*

Two tombstones of black granite, with neither wreaths nor flowers. On another child's tombstone I read these passionate woman's words: *He was greatly desired...* and then, nevertheless: *May God's will be done.*

We then walked toward Charonne, to inspect the little house where M. de Navailles died,[49] the house of M. de Saint-Cricq, the lovely poplars that border the end of his garden, and, behind the Père-Lachaise, those clusters of trees so prettily encircled amongst strawberry and rose bushes, between Charonne and Ménilmontant. In the middle, my two walnut trees, where I sat in 1819 with her, that stormy day. We then parted, I to go into M. de Saint-Cricq's house, she to return quickly to Paris, for the storm greatly frightened her. That was the beginning of our long union, stormy also, and yet so tender... She is buried at the same height as the two walnut trees, as well as I can judge, and with her are buried twenty years of my life, and the youth and sweetest emotions of my heart.

That spot is consecrated by one of Rousseau's *Reveries,* when he

48 She obtained a letter of recommendation from one of Michelet's former students at the Ecole normale, Pierre-Adolphe Chéruel (1809–91), who was teaching history in Rouen.

49 See chap. 1, n. 38.

took that sad and sweet walk there that ended so badly for him.[50] I too, walking across these same places, I feel "my soul still full of living feelings and my spirit still adorned with a few flowers."

7 June 1840, Sunday of Pentecost
It was on 6 June 1839 that Pauline left for Passy. Poor Pauline possessed something rare since, by her care and devotion, she saved the lives of her daughter in 1825, her husband in 1826–27, her son in 1832. Thus all that remains of her must forever be valued inestimably by her loved ones. I even kept the envelopes of my letters, which she had numbered and dated as she received them during my travels.

* * *

THE FECUNDITY OF DEATH (1840–1841) – Michelet continued to be torn apart. Marriage had seemed incompatible with his destiny as France's prophetic guide: "Such a task allows sharing neither one's time nor one's strength. I must live and die like a book, not like a man," he lamented on 23 June 1840. His uncharacteristic ascetic stance tried to subjugate intimate longings, for the widower's sexual fantasies disturbed his concentration. In the same entry he agreed with Edgar Quinet's wife, with whom he had discussed these matters frankly, that he should avoid going to bed with Marie, the family cook. She was his "black angel," carnal temptation. Michelet feared to repeat his disappointment with Pauline: "The most serious consequence of those half-marriages is that, alas! we love and commit ourselves completely to a person of inferior education, and from whom we will always be divorced in mind, who can love you only too little, to your sorrow, or too much, to hers."

The historian postponed the inevitable through study, travel, and his chaste friendship with Mme Dumesnil, his "white angel." He made an important trip to Belgium and the Ardennes region of France from 25 July to 16 August 1840. (He left Paris the day after the one-year anniversary of Pauline's death.) His travel *Journal* gen-

---

50 See chap. 1, n. 37.

erously described paintings, architecture, landscapes, conversations, and historical reflections. His second Collège de France course on the Renaissance began on 21 December 1840, and volumes 5 and 6 of the *History of France* appeared in August 1841 and January 1844, respectively. In an undated *Journal* entry of 1841 he exclaimed: "Yes, I want to swim in the Renaissance."

Michelet continued to mourn Pauline unfalteringly, especially in these final entries from 1841. With tragic eloquence he will consolidate his prophetic conception of history writing, which became his "second wife." By then grief was methodical, a "violent mental chemistry"; bereavement catalyzed a process of literary creation. Prolonged mourning placed his destiny before him: He examined it, pieced it together, and reinterpreted his own life. A revelation will integrate his fragmented selves. The Paris Panthéon—the secular burial place of Voltaire and Rousseau—will illumine his past. The Père-Lachaise cemetery had helped him visualize recent political events and conceive of history as autobiography. Now the Panthéon will organize the historian's own story.

2 March 1841, Tuesday

The *second wife* plays an important role in Indian dramas. She appears as jealousy and turmoil with regard to the first wife. She appears to the man as pleasure, *sui conscia* [self-aware], exquisite but all the more absorbing. The *second wife* (and I mean by that all those added to the first) is the true cause of the Asian's premature exhaustion, his inaction.

My *second wife*, history, appeared before 1830. My first wife, poor Pauline, was quite neglected. Because of that, everything that followed...

Toward the end of that ten-year period, my individuality often made demands. It leaned toward the black angel. My white angel forced me to save time. And now the black angel is decidedly elsewhere.

Thus the invincible will, hidden energy, chance or Providence, desire that nothing in me be given over to the individual life, that I no longer be a man, but a book.

* * *

11 March 1841, Thursday

Père-Lachaise. Visit to Pauline with my son; I explain his mother's epitaph to him. My daughter is at Mme Quinet's home. Sudden and hot spring, after the harshest winter since 1829, hot, scorching, but bare: leafless trees. I am boundless compared with 1829, but then I was complete. Today I feel myself like this leafless immensity: immense, it is true, but that makes it much easier to see the tombstones.

Also today, this morning, I finished the very difficult and complex outline of the last hundred pages of volume 5 (house of Bony, Gavre, etc., labor in the Middle Ages).[51] I think I endowed it with more morality, more intimacy. I attempted to do justice to things that have been condemned by time.

My method, but more intimate than that of 1 March (the latter wrenched my heart: to love):

1. Sympathy with those diverse nationalities, while at the same time condemning an incurable discord. Flemish mysticism: Béghardi, Ruysbroeck, A. Kempis. Then, after the disenchantment, the fatalism of Jansenius in the ruins of Ypres. Harshness, compared to Rubens. Practical wisdom of the Ardennes region, of Franche-Comté, of Savoie; violence and goodwill of Liège. Serious Dutch, endowed with extreme tenacity, slowness; serious childhood of the Frise region, which remains poetry: *Frisia non cantat.* [Friesland does not sing.]

2. Sympathy for solitary work, for the weavers, within their darkness, consoled by God. And I, too, by imitation. I am one of them. Sympathy for the happy and gentle work within families. I, too, knew it, when my home was not yet shattered. But after solitary work, family work, work in corporate bodies completed the harmony, and

51 This book covers the years 1364–1415 and includes the legend of Joan of Arc.

above all the associations pealed the bells, the great voice of public peace that harmonized everything. Only the weaver prayed, the father and mother made their children kneel. Everyone, without seeing one another, prayed together.

3. Finally, sympathy for the true, the great homeland, which comes to replace the commune, for true centralization, for France (abbreviate the mockery of false centralization).

13 March 1841, Saturday

Election of Thierry.[52] I had M. Guizot near me, and in front of me Dunot (Franche-Comté). "—What are you doing there?" M. Guizot asked me. "—I am looking for the life of a man whom no biography mentions and who, in the sixteenth century, ruled an empire."[53]

14 March 1841, Sunday

One of the first beautiful days, like one two years ago, while she was still alive, when we went out together for the last time and went to Passy where she was to die. Today I feel poorer than last year. Then I had moral vigor in addition: my pain, my recent loss.

25 March 1841, Thursday

Lived forty-two years, taught fifty years. From 1820 to 1827 at the collèges; from 1827 to 1835 at the Ecole normale. And, in my studies, lived fifty centuries... Nevertheless, it would be regrettable to finish already, when I was just beginning to abandon the simple straight line, but rather go simultaneously in three dimensions.

April 1841 (no specific date)

My grief is like my ring. At her death, I placed it on my finger, and

52 Amédée Thierry was elected to the historical section of the Académie des sciences morales to replace the deceased Baron Bignon.

53 Probably Nicolas Perrenot de Granvelle (1468–1555), chancellor of Charles V.

I thought it would be hard to get used to. Habit came, but the mark as well. When my turn comes, when they remove the ring, I will bear the deep groove it gave me.

4 April 1841, Palm Sunday

I need to prove to myself, to myself and to this humanity whose ephemeral appearances I sketch, to prove that we are reborn, that we do not die. I need to do it because I feel myself dying. It does no good for me to inventory the serious comforts of my present situation. I really hold onto life only out of my capacity, such as it is, to vivify something, to give life, in my manner.

So I want, above and beyond the chain of these mobile lives, to partake of those instants we call men, those sparkling little tales that were persons. I want to weave a fabric of the ideas by which they perpetuated themselves, continued to live, contradicted death, defied nature.

Nature weaves and tears, it knots, it breaks the living threads. We extract from ourselves, from our will, what we need in order to restore the bleeding fabric.

Let no one ask me why I seem to stop sometimes, to interrupt the human narrative, which breaks off every instant, to trace briefly a narrative of ideas.[54] It is because the ephemeral wearies me. It is because when my marionettes annoy me I throw them under the table. I set them aside to see if, at the very least, those hapless playthings ever had anything lasting within them. Or else I open them up and look to see whether or not their inner lives are the same under their different faces, whether or not they possess the same heart.

[54] Michelet was often criticized for adding too much legend or philosophy to his historical descriptions. Agronomist Adrien de Gasparin (1783–1862), minister of the interior of the Guizot government, wrote to Michelet in 1842, shortly after his Joan of Arc (*History of France*, vol. 5) appeared: "You are still an excellent narrator... But at the same time you are a man of imagination, a man who excessively tries to put facts into a mythical system, one which not everyone can accept."

Yes, it really was the same, and the same as mine: I suffer as they suffered.

Fecundity of death. Every system contains an internal conflict that maintains its life and prepares its maturity, its death, its fruit. Every system succeeds in releasing its fruit only by dying. That is a beautiful reason for dying: *Non causam vivendi* but *moriendi* [Not a reason for living but for dying].

For example, feudalism attained its beauty only when it stopped being feudalism: Enguerrand VII of Coucy. Feudalism contained within itself the civilized, refined war, whose dream produced chivalry: regularized war, shortened by tactics, in a word, war waged with the arts and spirit of peace (Turenne).

Which leads one to believe that, to be oneself to the highest degree, one must no longer be oneself but die, be transformed.

The Church, similarly, fulfills itself as church only when it has produced the mystics who consume it: Grace burns the Law. Royalty, similarly, obtains its noblest characteristic, irresponsibility, impeccability, only when it becomes a less absolute royalty, constitutional monarchy. Rome (and Montesquieu in his *Grandeur and Decadence* did not understand this)[55] was not truly Rome, that is, the boundless city, the city of humankind, until it opened its gates to the world and seemed to be less Rome. Its decadence as a city was its fulfillment, its fruit as civilization. Montesquieu was pained to see Caesar, Claudius, summon the Gauls, to see each province represented in Rome by an emperor, Spain by Trajan, Gaul by Antonius, Arabia by..., Syria by Alexander Severius, etc. He did not notice that bringing the world into Rome, first by the slaves and captives (see Scipio Emilian's speech to the people: *Noverca est...* [The step-

[55] Charles de Secondat, baron de Montesquieu (1689–1755), the outstanding political philosopher, published *Considerations on the Causes of the Grandeur of the Romans and Their Decadence* in 1734; his celebrated *Spirit of the Laws* appeared in 1748.

mother is...]), then by the jurisconsults (Papinian, Ulpian), who were more Roman than Rome itself, —that this concentration is the fulfillment of the true Rome. See Saint-Augustine.

29 April 1841, Thursday
At the Feuillantine bath, nine o'clock.

I found myself again at the same place as in June 1839, the eve of my wife's death, and I recalled my painful impression of inner misery and abandonment. Only the bitter observations of Saint-Simon[56] could distract me a bit. I was dead and I felt, within that death, life protesting by violent shooting pains in the heart.

It was then that I questioned why my hard existence, completely devoted to the benefit of others, had had no recompense. I complained about it. To whom? Not to God, for I barely felt Him any longer. I said to myself from time to time: As bare and ravaged as He has made me, He could deprive me of more, afflict my father, my children. I should be tactful, appease that terrible power, bless it. I cannot do it.

My wife died and my heart was torn to pieces. But from that very sundering a violent and almost delirious energy emerged: I plunged with a dark pleasure into the death of France in the fifteenth century, blending with it those fiercely sensual passions that I found equally in myself and in my subject. Not without truth someone wrote that the fourth volume was engendered by an immoral inspiration.[57] That is what makes its strange power. Never has a bad epoch been narrated with worse mental distress.

---

56 Louis de Rouvroy, duc de Saint-Simon (1675–1755), served in the courts of Louis XIII, Louis XIV, and Louis XV. After the regent's death in 1723, he wrote incisive and detailed *Mémoires*, first published in 1829–30.

57 Michelet alludes to an article in the Catholic paper *L'Univers* (26 May 1840), in which Abbé Douhaire criticized the historian's impassioned evocation of the dances of death in volume 4 of the *History of France*. Michelet's former pupil at the Collège Sainte-Barbe, the Catholic Alfred Nettement (1805–65), deplored the volume's "pantheism" in the *Gazette de France* (February 1840).

One thing made my heart wither and turned it against the world: that my teaching, as intimate and sincere as it was, always benevolent, should have produced nothing for my happiness. As for my rivals' hatred, the malevolence of the powerful, I easily found solace for that. But the fact that I found so little attachment, often little sincerity, among my students, at most a pleasant relationship, a cold friendship —that was harsh for me.

That treasure of life that I poured forth so widely for twenty years and from which I could have fertilized ten times more books than I have written, those floods of running water that had gushed from my heart for so long, —where have they gone, I said to myself. Have they flowed into sterile sand? What! My life flowed out of me and no one gathered it...

9 June 1841, Wednesday
The Panthéon, which people say such bad things about and which is nonetheless an austere and sublime temple, appeared three times to me, at three periods of my life.

1818. —The first time, I was sixteen years old. I was walking alone in the Jardin des Plantes in stormy weather. I climbed to the labyrinth and, from there, I saw the entire south wrapped in black clouds... Then, suddenly, that curtain opened. The sun, which was hidden, appeared, dazzling, in the windows of the dome. That great light, whose source was hidden, seemed an illumination of a mysterious Eleusinian temple, a sudden transfiguration of glory, of life to come. Everything great and good that such a light, dazzling in the majesty of such an artistic monument of art, can promise...

1839. —Twenty years pass, and I reach, after numerous sorrows, many works, my solitude during these last years, a period in which I felt increasingly more appealing, perhaps more worthy of being liked, and in which I nonetheless anticipated a progressive isolation. Precisely because I was at my height, each day it became less probable that I would encounter what Shakespeare said: "Just as high as my heart."[58] I returned home sadly, therefore, one foggy evening, enveloped even more by the fog of my thoughts. But above the dark mists towered the calm, cold, melancholy head of my favorite giant... I who had seen it during my first vision so glowing, so filled with sun and hope, now I found it even more sublime but quite pitiful. This time it represented to me the genius of knowledge, the dreaming and calculating genius of modern thought, hovering in its solitude.

—*This very day*, I had the third vision. I connected the Panthéon to an image of my entire life, if not completed, at least crowned. I recalled how my harsh childhood had climbed, with effort and ripping fingernails, those great, steep walls that rise a hundred feet without foothold. I recalled my maturity.

18 June 1841, Friday

History: violent mental chemistry, where my individual passions evolve into generalities, where my generalities become passions, where my peoples become me, where my self returns to vivify the peoples.

They appeal to me so that I will make them live. Alas! Am I really alive? Oh, brothers, I do not lack compassion, it is boundless and painful. But do you believe I can untangle your grief from mine? I willingly take it into myself. But won't I confuse them? Will my individual life not take the place of your general life?

Then they said to me, lamenting, that it was the same thing, that they and I were but one, that our hearts suffered in the same way, that their life lived in my life, that these pale phantoms were my phantom, or rather that I myself was the living, fleeting phantom of peoples fixed in real existence and in changelessness.

* * *

58 From *As You Like It*, act 3, scene 2, line 268.

24 July 1841, Saturday

Second anniversary of Pauline's death. At 9:00 a.m. we all go to church. Mme Dumesnil consoles the father and the daughter. In the service for the dead, the passages taken from Job are badly translated, that is, in the Christian manner and from the perspective of resignation.[59] [. . .]

59 See Alfred Dumesnil's letter to Eugène Noël, quoted in the commentary that begins chapter 3.

3 The Death of My White Angel

FRANÇOISE-ADÈLE FANTELIN DUMESNIL
12 January 1799–31 May 1842

– My role as dreamer and nursemaid, during this beautiful and chilly month of May, among the faded lilacs, during the advancing year, was not without poetry. Harsh poetry in the presence of death!
Journal, 9 May 1842 –

– Death soon threatened Michelet's faith again. By February 1841 his first female intellectual companion, Mme Dumesnil, had moved from Rouen to Paris for medical treatment. When, in August, her illness was diagnosed as a malignant tumor (of the womb or the cervix), the dying woman moved into the historian's home on the rue des Postes. His daughter Adèle became her nurse. Their household was again harrowed by death. The *Journal* of 1842 chronicles the battle between love and anticipatory mourning.

Since the previous summer Michelet had known that his "white angel" was dying of cancer, and this gifted, bereaved woman aroused his deepest yearnings. Adèle Fantelin had a long history of distress. She was born in 1799 and in 1816 married a Rouen banker and land speculator, Ferdinand-Emilien Poullain-Dumesnil (1771–1868), thirty-eight years of age. This lovely, refined person of seventeen could share none of her inner life with this prosaic, insensitive man. Her first four children died, and when Alfred was born in 1821 motherhood became the focus of her existence.

Mother and son lived together at Vascoeuil, her ancestral property in Normandy, or at a country house near Rouen called the Sente-Bihorel, until Alfred went to Paris to study law, as did most provincial young men of good breeding. Alfred had more independence and attended courses on art history, philosophy, and history and became enthralled with Michelet's exciting lectures at the Collège de France. He urged his mother to join him in the capital. Mme Dumesnil, already separated from her husband, came to Paris in 1839 and sat beside her son in the university amphitheater. The Dumesnil and the Michelet families would soon become one.

The historian first welcomed the young Dumesnil into his home in November 1839. Alfred had been recommended by one of Michelet's favorite students at the Ecole normale, Pierre-Adolphe Chéruel, who taught history in Rouen. Chéruel had traveled with his professor to England in 1834, and his letter was taken seriously. Alfred soon felt comfortable, while his mother appreciated Michelet's courses and wrote him several letters. But the two adults did not meet face to face until May 1840. Their relations were cordial but distant.

The historian remained surprisingly reserved even when he received Mme Dumesnil on 5 May 1840.[1] His wife's death seemed to discourage him from accepting her gracious invitations to spend an evening at the apartment she shared with her son on the rue Taitbout. One of his letters explains why:

> I rarely go out, especially in the evening. Since my loss, I have completely become a preceptor and a governess; it is hard for me to leave my children. My seclusion is so strict that I have broken off all relationships. I almost no longer see my oldest friend, with whom I was a student[2] and who lives on the same street. I have little time, and I also fear to sadden those who care about me. Excuse me therefore, Madam, if I cannot go to see you.
>
> Madam, you put it quite well: the study of history is stormy and sad. It is even more so in my particular situation. My double sadness demands solitude. Wounded animals act instinctively: they are patient and hide. Time heals them sometimes. I hope that this avowal can justify my poor responses to your flattering letters, for which I am deeply grateful.

Something happened during the week after their first encounter. Mme Dumesnil had informed Michelet of Alfred's delicate health and asked him to guide his career. She was gratified that he advised her to remain near her son. Here is how she described the historian's return visit on 17 May in a letter to Alfred, who remained in Rouen:

> I received M. Michelet's visit. He was extremely friendly to me. He told me about his courses and asked me if I found them useful and beneficial to people who need to be encouraged. His intentions are quite lofty and extremely moral; finally, he spoke to me with so much appreciation that I felt unworthy. But since he almost constantly spoke about himself, I could not stop the flow of conversation to discuss you as I had wished. When I left him, I expressed my gratitude for the attention of a person whose time is so precious. He answered that it was a real need for him, a duty and especially a pleasure, and he was happy to find me home...

From the very beginning, Mme Dumesnil perceived Michelet's com-

1 See above, entry of 24 May 1840 and note 48 (chap. 2).
2 Hector Poret; see above, entry of 21 February 1821 and note 11 (chap. 1).

bination of seductiveness, self-centeredness, and generous concern. Their friendship started on a realistic note. Mme Dumesnil then returned to Normandy before moving to Paris in February 1841. She had undergone medical treatment in Rouen but now needed the experts. In Paris, she and Michelet soon deepened their love and contracted a sort of "secret marriage." He had reconstituted his family.

The exact nature of their relationship remains a mystery. However, one thing is certain: Michelet admired the cultured and witty Mme Dumesnil as he had admired no other woman and he enthusiastically shared his thoughts and feelings with her. She wore an iron ring to mark their partnership, although, officially, she was still married. We have no direct evidence of any sexual relations—not in the *Journal*, nothing in letters, and no comments from other family members. (The second Mme Michelet, whom the historian married in 1849, jealous of her new possession, certainly must have urged her husband to destroy pages of the *Journal* relating to their closeness.) What remains are his suggestions, after Mme Dumesnil's death, that he did not receive all he desired.[3] Whatever the facts, Mme Dumesnil's rapidly developing cancer of the reproductive organs must have discouraged physical intimacies.

Michelet did in fact get what he truly wanted, although all too briefly. He longed for communion more than for sexual gratification. Her cancer did not destroy their spiritual bond. The two families were united by June 1841 when Alfred and his mother left their little apartment and came to live with Michelet, his children, and his father on the rue des Postes. A long letter that Alfred wrote to his closest friend in Normandy, Eugène Noël, soon after moving, typified their communal life and revealed the historian's closeness to Alfred, who became another son:

> My mother is still quite weak. And her treatments are so painful that, while they cure the local ill, her nervous system remains shattered after one of those agonizing operations.[4]
>
> But her mind is quite vigorous and she is confident about the

[3] See below, entries of 15 June, 14 and 21 September 1842.

[4] Mme Dumesnil's cervical or uterine tumor was periodically cauterized.

future. M. Michelet and I often fence with that fearsome talker. I can tell you, because you can understand, never have two minds been more united than ours, never have broader and more intimate sympathies existed between two educated men and of such different ages. But he, he is all ages; and I, if I lack intelligence and experience, at least I possess fervor and enthusiasm for ideas. [. . .]

Yesterday, at lunch, M. Michelet looked at the six of us and said: "It is a perfect lyre." I must tell you how we were placed at table when we had no guests, and were happier. It is a round table like yours, large enough only for six. In the middle, M. Michelet (to the west); toward the north, my mother, then M. Michelet's father; Mlle Michelet[5] to the east, right in front of her father (that is essential, for M. Michelet likes symmetry); then me next to her, in front of my mother; and Charles next to me and his father and facing his grandfather. That is the best arrangement: I have the eyes of my mother and M. Michelet and my two little friends next to me. [. . .]

The letter continued with a vivid picture of the historian's busy life, his work habits, and the richness of his social and intellectual relations; it is the most detailed description that we possess:

I tell you that in ten days M. Michelet will publish his fifth volume, after which we will visit either Versailles or Fontainebleau. He has never been in more complete or rapid movement. He compares himself to a railway, but a railway from which age-old oak trees can be seen two hundred feet below. Once launched in his history of the nineteenth century [*sic*], he will associate us intimately with his daily work, through readings and conversations. His activity is prodigious and he writes a lot. For the past two months, besides his fifth volume, he has written a book on historical method that will not be published; he is collecting materials and documents relating to the French Revolution. He maintains a frantic correspondence: packets of letters arrive at

5 Adèle was sixteen and Charles eleven at the time.

all hours of the day, and he answers every one. Every fact interests him; he involves himself with all of us with such attentive concern that he knows not only all our little acts but also our thoughts. At the same time he docs favors for many people. Nothing is too much—errands, visits, and letters. He goes to the Archives every day, and, from 3:00 p.m. to 10:30 p.m., he receives visitors, converses, goes for walks, in fact he appears to have nothing to do.

To give you an example, here is what we did yesterday. At 9:00 a.m. we all went to the service that M. Michelet has celebrated every year for his wife's death.[6] M. Michelet had already worked all morning, and, following the routine he established at Rouen, after having taken coffee at 7:00 a.m., he had come to wish my mother good morning (you remember that). When we returned from church, M. Michelet asked me to join him in his study, where he analyzed with me prayers for the dead taken from the Book of Job. He showed me how much the French version printed in the prayerbook was inaccurate, even deceptive (notice also that the prayer added between the bold biblical verses softens their effect). We ate lunch; lunch and dinner are devoted to family. At lunch we share all our thoughts about the morning and night, at dinner everything we saw during the day.

At 11:00 a.m. M. Michelet left for the Stock Exchange and Law Courts for a litigation in which he was named with MM. Nodier and Tissot.[7] He returned at 12:30 p.m., and we went to see M. Ingres's painting of "The Virgin," which you have probably heard about.[8] M. Ingres had invited M. Michelet in a letter I have right before me. He received us in person at his home, and

---

6 See above, entry of 24 July 1841.

7 Charles Nodier (1780–1844) was a prolific author who, as librarian at the Arsenal during the 1820s, hosted the first gatherings of the Romantic movement. Pierre-François Tissot (1768–1854), member of the Académie française, participated in the 1789 Revolution, translated Virgil, and wrote poetry and books on history and literature.

8 Jean-Auguste-Dominique Ingres (1780–1867) was the master of an approach to painting that put "classical" line before "romantic" color. His portraits and paintings of the female figure are superlative.

we could understand the work by knowing the painter. I don't have time now to share my thoughts, and one should devote more than a few sentences to such matters. While the women bought bonnets in a store, we shared our impressions of the painter and the painting. After we returned, M. Michelet had a long business conference, then came to show me the books his binder had delivered. My mother and I chatted with the book binder [. . .]. We let M. Michelet work and read M. Quinet's book, *Germany and Italy,*[9] which I am reading to my mother and Mademoiselle...

Then M. de Müller, minister of justice at Weimar, came for dinner. He lived with Goethe (they spent evenings together for more than twenty years); he knew intimately Napoleon, Wieland, Herder, Schiller. Also Baudry,[10] near whom I was placed at table and with whom I became quite personal, for we spoke about languages, about the influence of Orientalist studies on world history. That study throws so much light on antiquity and the Middle Ages! M. Quinet arrived at dessert time. Can you imagine what the conversation became? M. de Müller spoke about his diplomatic career; M. Quinet told us about his travels. M. Michelet was dazzling. Then a young man, M. Louis Batissier, was announced; he had spent two weeks in Rouen, where he was sent to write a review of the exposition for the *Journal de Rouen*. He wrote an essay on Géricault. Read the articles "Eleusis" and "Vie de Lasueur" that appeared in the *Revue des deux mondes* on 15 July. M. Quinet recommended them.

I am living in M. Michelet's house on the third floor. Two rooms with a magnificent view of the countryside... You must stay here when you come to Paris....

The renewed family celebrated their union despite the pall of Mme Dumesnil's illness. Together they enjoyed the evenings, singing

---

[9] Edgar Quinet, who had become particularly close to Alfred, published *Allemagne et Italie* in 1839, a study of history, politics, art, literature, and philosophy.

[10] Frédéric Baudry, a young man from Normandy recommended by Chéruel to accompany Michelet on his trip to Switzerland and Italy in July 1838. Baudry entered the Ecole normale the following year, studied Oriental languages, and became the head of the Arsenal library in 1859.

French and German folk songs and excitedly discussing their readings and thoughts. Michelet and his children, with Mme Dumesnil and Alfred, vacationed in the Fontainebleau forest from 13 to 17 August and visited Mme Dumesnil's home at Vascoeuil from 24 August to 5 September. Everyone shared the pleasures of companionship as well as anxieties about the sick woman's health and financial problems. The terminally ill person might be forced to sell her property. The two families identified so much with each other that, on 19 December 1841, Michelet's *Journal* recorded that Charles dreamt that the Sente-Bihorel would be taken.

Michelet attempted to mitigate these future losses by expanding his optimistic historical vision. Mme Dumesnil's cancer forced him to reformulate his philosophy of life and death. He completed volume 5 of the *History of France* (the reign of Charles VII, with Joan of Arc), which went on sale 23 August 1841. The brief preface to volume 4, dated 1840, had reflected Pauline's recent demise: "Both this and the following volume examine the crisis of the fifteenth century, the two phases of that crisis when France appeared to destroy itself. This volume recounts its death, the next one its resurrection." Michelet's morbid enthusiasm for the dances of death in the fourth volume was counterbalanced by his adulation of the heroic Maid of Orleans in the fifth volume. This historical sequence of death and resurrection was also the author's own odyssey.

THE SILENCES OF HISTORY

The *Journal*'s most elevated accents arose from this cruel conflict of agony and hope. Michelet reenacted the ancient mystery of poetry born of bereavement as his lyrical prose took wing. He wrote at the bedside of the slowly dying woman who inspired him. By January 1842—when our selections resume—Michelet acknowledged that the doctors Lisfranc and Patin could not improve her condition. They consulted still another expert, the German homeopathic physician Frederic Hahnemann (1755–1843), a leading specialist. The following entry of 30 January 1842 will raise mourning to its highest creative level as the historian asserts his oracular power to "make the silences of history speak." The poet-prophet armed with the Golden Bough of compassion, like Virgil's Aeneas who penetrated the ghostly kingdom, would endow his nation's past with eternal life.

19 January 1842, Wednesday
Wrote some of the preface to the sixth volume on method. My France will pardon me for having dared hang my swallow's nest on its monument, that I want to be so noble and lofty.

20 January 1842, Thursday
The last day that I tended the sick woman [. . .].

30 January 1842, Sunday
This entire week, quite intimate, few or no events. Mme Dumesnil increasingly ill. I keep Alfred at my house during the mornings. In the evening, M. Couture,[11] who wanted to finish both portraits before 20 February, came several times. The twenty-sixth, Wednesday evening, the piano restored her taste for music. She sang all evening.

In urna perpetuum ver [In the urn, perpetual springtime]. Plutarch relates that Caesar, while he was navigating one day between..., fell asleep and dreamt that he saw an entire army in tears, a multitude of men weeping and beseeching him. When he awoke, he wrote on his tablets: *Corinth* and *Carthage*. And he rebuilt those two cities.[12]

---

11 The academic painter Thomas Couture (1815–79) was a socialist with whom Michelet became friends around 21 August 1841, when Couture began portraits of the historian and Mme Dumesnil. The portrait of Michelet (now at the Musée Carnavalet) was rejected for the Salon of 1843 but accepted in 1847.

12 From Plutarch, *Life of Caesar*, 57. Michelet recounts this "dream" in his autobiographical preface to *The People* in 1846; it dates from at least 1840, according to the entry of 30 September 1842, which relates it to another problem.

His grandson, the emperor Claudius, did more. He did not rebuild the cities, but he tried to remake the peoples themselves, to renew them through history. Leaving Rome and the Empire to his slaves, he became the emperor of the dead, of the demolished world. With his hands he patiently scraped up what dust remained of Etruria, Tyre, Carthage, warmed as best he could those pitiful ashes, and, wanting at least the name to remain, he established a chair at the Museum of Alexandria and a perpetual reader to teach.

The historian is neither Caesar nor Claudius. But in his dreams he often sees a throng weeping and lamenting, a multitude of those who do not have enough, who want to live again. That multitude is everyone, humanity. Tomorrow, we will be part of it.

Men of a hundred years, nations of two thousand years, children dead at the breast, they all say that they have hardly lived, they have barely begun —that, like Jephthah's daughter,[13] they were given only one month to cry before dying. They say that, if they had had the time to know themselves and prepare, they might have accepted their lot, they would have ceased wandering thus around us, they would have let us gently close their urns. Cradled by friendly hands, they would have gone back to sleep and resumed their dreams.

—But what! When you were still in that warm light, when you possessed your little moment, when you lived, loved, suffered like us, why didn't you try to make what you cherished endure, to endow your meager infinity of a day with infinite duration?

—"We died, still stammering. Our pitiful chronicles confirm that enough. We did not realize mankind's sovereign attribute, the distinct, clear voice that alone explains, consoles by explaining...

---

13 In the Book of Judges (chap. 11), Jephthah was a Gileadite warrior. He vowed to sacrifice the first person he saw upon returning home if God would accord him victory over the Ammonites. His only child, a daughter, came to greet him. She mourned for two months—not only one, as Michelet states—before she was sacrificed. Alfred de Vigny wrote a touching poem on this story.

And if we had had a voice, could we have expressed life? We did not know how."

May someone come who knows us better than we ourselves do, to whom God has given a heart and ears to hear, from the earth's depths, the sad, shrill voice and the feeble breath, someone who loves the dead, who will find and speak to them the very words they never speak, words that remained to be spoken and still lie heavy in the coffin.

Yes, it is not only an urn for which they ask with tears and prayers. It is not a funeral chant, a woman paid to weep. They want a seer, a *vates:*

> Sed non ante datur telleris operta subire
> Auricomos quam quis decerpserit arbore foetus.
> Hoc sibi pulchra suum ferri Proserpina munus
> Instituit...
>
> [But one is forbidden to enter the secret places of the earth before one has plucked the golden-haired branch from the tree. The beautiful Persephone has ordered that this her gift be returned to her.][14]

We must have the Golden Bough. From where can we pluck it? From our own heart. Through his personal sorrows the historian absorbs and reproduces the sorrows of nations; renews them in order to soothe them.

But not only do those dead call for an urn and tears. They would not be satisfied if we simply renew their sighs. They do not need a funeral chant, a woman paid to weep, but a seer, a *vates*. Until they possess that seer, they shall roam around their badly closed graves and will not rest.

They need an Oedipus who will solve their own riddles, whose

[14] Virgil, *The Aeneid*, book 6, lines 140–44.

meaning they do not know, who will teach them what their words, their acts—which they do not understand—signify. They need a Prometheus. And when he has stolen the fire, the icy voices that float in the air will come together, produce sounds, begin speaking again. We need more. We must hear the words that were never spoken, which remained in the depths of hearts (excavate yours, they are there). We must make the silences of history speak, those fearsome organ pauses when history speaks no more and which are precisely its most tragic tones.

Only then do the dead accept the sepulcher. They begin to understand their destiny and gather its agonizing dissonances into a softer harmony, to say to each other, very quietly, Oedipus's final words: *pántōs gàr ékhei táde kûros* [Everything has been fulfilled].[15] The shades are soothed and appeased. They allow their urns to be closed again. They go away, cradled by friendly hands, go back to sleep, and resume their dreams. Precious urn of times past, the pontiffs of history bear it and pass it on to each other, with such pity, with such tender care! (no one knows it better than they themselves), as if they were bearing the ashes of their father and their son. But is it not themselves?

4 February 1842, Friday

I set seriously to work again on *Louis XI*, on reading Legrand, for 1465, etc.[16]

She seemed a bit better, she could sit, she didn't hear the loud noise during the night. Yesterday I bought a picture of Normandy. This morning, beautiful sun, February spring. But she could not go out because she had taken her bath. I spoke to Alfred about put-

15 The final verse of Sophocles' *Oedipus at Colonnus*.

16 Michelet examines the Legrand manuscripts at the Bibliothèque royale as he prepares the notes for volume 6 of the *History of France*.

ting the Saint-Ouen Church[17] in the background of her portrait. He answered quite wisely that neither Rouen nor Vascoeuil were necessary, but nothing or the rue des Postes. I had thought of Van Dyck d'Eu: Marie de Médicis. Antwerp...

At night, painful dream, which related somewhat to her unpleasant business about Vascoeuil. Effort to be free, to reclaim my personality. Yesterday I compared that effort to that of Ulysses, thrust upon the beach, repelled; his hands struggling. It is like the polyp which, dragged from its bed, keeps the pebbles in its torn filaments. (*The Odyssey E. sub fine* [Book 5. near the end].)

MADAME DUMESNIL'S SLOW AGONY

Michelet had successfully transmuted individual grief into an artistic method: "Through his personal sorrows the historian absorbs and reproduces the sorrows of nations." The writer subsumed all mythic heroes as he conquered mortality with his pen. He was at once a Caesar who rebuilt cities, an Oedipus who deciphered the riddle of the Sphinx, and a rebellious Prometheus, a Titan who enflamed the God-challenging ambitions of civilization—a poet, interpreter, and revolutionary prophet. As a man of flesh and blood, however, Michelet lost control of the woman he loved. He became just another helpless victim of death.

Mme Dumesnil was a devout Catholic who confided in her confessor, Abbé Coeur,[18] an eloquent preacher and professor of sacred oratory and theology at the University of Paris. The priest respected Michelet and attended his courses. But when her cancer and the excruciating cauterizations had weakened Mme Dumesnil's normally buoyant spirit, the dying woman seemed to prefer this liberal Jesuit to her adopted "husband." Michelet felt angry at his beloved, despite

---

17 The cathedral in Rouen, begun around 1318 and completed in 1614. It included an important monastery.

18 Pierre-Louis Coeur was a renowned preacher who refused to support the ultramontane Jesuits seeking control of the university. He was decorated in 1840 by Louis-Philippe, and in November 1842 he received a chair in theology at the Sorbonne.

her mortal illness, but treasured every kind word. Desperately, he competed with Mme Dumesnil's professional helpers—her Catholic entourage and various healers who attempted to cure her—while his love persevered.

18 February 1842, Friday
Quid teaching (Tuileries...)? In the evening, Dargaud announces Abbé Coeur's visit for tomorrow.

19 February 1842, Saturday
I did not go to the Institut, still feeling gripped by chest pains. At four o'clock Abbé Coeur arrived, still deeply moved and trembling from his sermon at Saint-Séverin. He was badly informed. However, clever and tender: "Every situation has its stormy moments; under the most peaceful appearances..." I have since found out that she had spoken well of me, that even then she had remembered me, attesting to her wish that, if she were cured, she would devote herself to my family.

22 February 1842, Tuesday
M. Chatron had announced that he would bring Amussat,[19] for (. . .) the operation on her womb. He didn't come until Monday. He is the surgeon of Hahnemann, Récamier, Rostan. He considered amputation to be the only remedy for Mme Boivin.

Yesterday, Monday, Mme Cartier who, because Abbé Guerry was away, suggests Abbé Beauvais: thirty-six years old, a man of more heart than intellect. I was doubly hurt: everything escapes me... After the surgeons, she wanted a foreign hypnotist,[20] then the con-

19 Jean-Zuléma Amussat (1796–1856), one of the great surgeons of his time, confirmed the diagnosis of a malignant tumor. Chatron and the others were Michelet's regular doctors.

20 It was believed that magnetic passes (projection of the will) might help cure physical ailments.

fessor. In such crises the soul becomes distant from those who love it without effectively helping it. She seeks life from strangers, from foreigners. That, for me, is an unexpected form of death, to feel her confidence and affection dying. It is as if I myself were dying. How can I convey the feeling of that daily confiding of despair? And yet, when Amussat arrived, she said, trembling: "My fate will be decided."

24 February 1842, Thursday

Pale spring, with winter washed away, with your unhappy, odorless flowers, oh how dark you appear to me! In the middle of February, even those bird songs make me grieve. Why that leap toward life? *Quae lucis miseris tam dira cupido*? [What is that harsh desire for light that possesses those unhappy people?][21]

I had barely emerged from the night: I return to it, and from winter into winter: *from wintra in wintra*.[22] But into a permanent winter, the ice of age, ice of the heart. *Majores cadunt altis de montibus umbrae* [Longer shadows fall from high mountains]. I can say: *Tectorum culmina fumant*... [Rooftops are smoking.][23]

We should go thus, returning to the source of our regrets, striving to regain the many friends we met too late, whom we did not even meet.

Why not Byron? Why not Racine? Why not Shakespeare and Michelangelo? Why not Dante? Why not Virgil? A great family, friends, patrons, parents of my thought, why didn't we live at the same time? Oh puerile regret, useless childish sorrow!

21 Virgil, *The Aeneid*, book 6, line 721.

22 Michelet quotes this old English in a note to *The Bird* (1856) citing Augustin Thierry's *Conquest of England by the Normans*: "Of wintra in wintra cometh."

23 Michelet had cited these verses twice, in reverse order, on 23 September 1839, as he described a sunset on the Saint-Germain hills on returning to Paris from Normandy, shortly after Pauline's death: "The eventide of life arrives, still luminous, but already spread with huge cold shadows."

1 March 1842, Tuesday

For the first time, since long ago, I went to bed early. Neither reading nor hypnotism. It is the beginning of separation. I had chatted a bit after dinner. I had criticized her for not expressing gratitude to the Lécuyer's little maid who had visited and showed such a lively interest.

—"But," she said (a bit improved), "why depend upon people's feelings when you must detach yourself?"

—I answered: "And why detach yourself? We must harmonize feelings, not uproot them!"

Yesterday I saw Yanowski.[24] Today, M. Letronne advised me not to compromise his life at Easter time but rather to resume my teaching.

16 March 1842, Wednesday

Yesterday, Tuesday, after the Tuileries, after having posed for M. Couture, I saw her at five o'clock. She was talking very loudly, very clearly, in a desperate tone: "If this lasts," she said, "both of you will go through it too. Make me unconscious, and do with me what you wish..." Those words seemed so contrary to her character that I was shattered.

I said to Abbé Coeur: "It is as if I see the forest, above a treeless hill, that no longer keeps the waters back. The poor trees appear, their roots bare, tangled on the bottom, displaying to the daylight the sad branches made for night and that had never been seen."

This morning I decided to organize all my papers in a rigorously chronological order, so that all my knowledge might enter into my life.

24 Michelet's former student Jean Yanowski (1813–51) replaced him at the Collège de France in February for a single lecture. But he was soon stricken with a relapse of a pulmonary infection of which he would die in 1851. The administrator Letronne urged Michelet to relieve his ailing substitute.

17 March 1842, Thursday

I informed M. Letronne that I would give my course. I received visits from Mme Cartier's doctor, an old man, and from Abbé Coeur who stayed for three hours and gave her Communion. Held back by a sprain, I fruitlessly attempted to enter the room.

Yesterday I told Alfred that instead of isolating religions, instead of subdividing them—their influence on philosophy, influence on history, on poetry, etc.—Quinet should have quite simply linked them together by means of an inner idea.[25] He should have invented the religions one by one, drawing them out of his heart and asking each one: What remedy does this one provide to the soul? That study would have given his book what is missing: energy, continuity, progress.

* * *

THE DRAMA OF TRANSFIGURATION

–To fortify himself against death and diminish his identification with the dying woman, Michelet turned inward. Urgently, he imitated the cycle dramatized in the religious calendar. It was Easter, the season of death and resurrection. As the period of rebirth approached, the historian began to "revise" his "formula," reexamining his philosophy of history and theory of artistic resurrection in light of his past with Pauline. He attempted to support his faltering faith with meditations on Spinoza, Leibniz, and Hegel. Then he reread and analyzed his *Journal* from at least 1831 to the present, endeavoring to "reunite" his "fragments." In the following entry he will sketch a preliminary autobiography, partition his past into stages, and define each particular insight by the book that it produced. Love, loss, and intellectual progress were inseparable. There was another benefit: Grief revealed history to him "as if for the first time."

[25] Edgar Quinet had just published his philosophical and historical study, *Le Génie des religions*.

26 March 1842, Saturday

On 14 July 1839 everything became simplified. As my vague feelings of sadness turned into concrete pain, my afflicted heart recaptured its vigor.

For a long time now, I had dreamt of death. I had often planned to write a pastoral poem about the deceased: the cemetery as an intermediary existence between life and resurrection; new relationships between people who had not met; love affairs of the dead amidst the rose and the nightingale. See entry of 17 June 1831 in my garden (on rue de l'Arbalète),[26] after I published my *Roman History*. In 1837, walks in my garden (rue des Fossés-Saint-Victor), which became the burial ground of the doctrine.[27] In 1838, my project to renew all life through history, through all love, through all bereavement.

In 1837, as I was walking in my garden on the rue des Fossés-Saint-Victor, I had grasped the idea that life and death were nothing other than the synthesis and analysis of God; that in order to realize one's better self, one must no longer be oneself.

My philosophy, or disgust with an eternal analysis, had no power to reunite my fragments and brought me to a very low point, very low indeed, in October 1837, until 1839. During 1838–39, I wrote: *Vitamque perosi projecere animas* [Those who through hatred of life have rejected life].[28] In 1838 my trip to Venice had lifted my spirits; but in 1839 my trip to Lyon had not done so.

I was wasting away, stretched out over a vast surface like a swamp, without finding my flow. That violent shock compelled me to extend myself into the depths and dig into my soul. I grasped life,

---

26 Michelet lived on rue de la Roquette from 1818 to 1827; on the rue de l'Arbalète from 1827 to 1831; on the rue des Fossés-Saint-Victor from 1831 to 1836; and on the rue des Postes from 1836 to 1849.

27 See above, entry of 7 February 1837 and note 42 (chap. 1).

28 Virgil, *The Aeneid*, book 6, lines 435–36. Michelet paraphrases the text: "*lucemque perosi / Projecere animas*" (those who through hatred of *light*).

all that it includes as individual, deplorable, irreparable. I grasped death and everything in it that is fertile and enduring. In other words, history appeared to me as if for the first time.

A thousand simultaneous points of view:

—First, the fury of the flesh, in life and in death (the entire fourth volume of the *History of France* translates this insight), the blind passion of the dog dying at its master's tomb, the powerful attraction to the grave (Inès de Castro). I clung to the dictum of Leibniz, that the soul cannot survive without a body.

—Then, everything that is irretrievable in individuality that truly appears only once; nothing like it before, nothing after. We love because of the shortcomings themselves, and that is perhaps what justifies death. The badly loved person must perish, since love, which equates him with the good, would otherwise perpetuate him.

Fecundity, vitality of death, for mankind and for systems, such I had conceived of death in 1838. Death sorts out, it sifts; that is, it removes the evil, sets free the good, so that it will endure. Death guarantees true perpetuity, the true life.

But, in that less good and less true part, which perishes as individual, there had been life, which is beneficial at least as a cause. That fact should hallow in our memories those who have prepared the way for us. Respect for the past, tender respect!

Thus an intimate bond of affection links all the ages. Just as Marcus Aurelius, when he began his career, thanked each of his tutors for each virtue, how could I not thank each century for the powers within me?

27 March 1842, Easter Sunday

A strange thing, my ideas are the events of my life. Alongside of such a painful reality, but because of that reality, these days I stubbornly worked to transform my formula.

* * *

– Guiding Michelet's development was the Feast of the Ascension, which celebrated Christ's rise into heaven forty days after the Resurrection. Holy Thursday, or Ascension Day, would fall on 5 May 1842. Between Easter Sunday and 9 May Michelet continued to reconsider his theories in long, intricate entries and in daily conversations with Alfred Dumesnil. The historian ripened his ideas in private lessons to the ruling family and in the seven lectures on the philosophy of history, presented between 7 April and 26 May at the Collège de France. Both teaching and writing struggled with the problem of extinction. Was Nature a benign or hostile mother? He asked quite boldly in an undated *Journal* entry of April: "If she is a mother, then why is there death? [. . .] Finally I told myself: Death must be a childbirth. Irrefutably, it must be."

The historian shared the belief of many nineteenth-century thinkers that death included a series of reincarnations. During those weeks of intense speculation and doubt, Michelet found solace in the writings of Pierre Leroux,[29] Eugène Burnouf's renderings of Hindu philosophy, and the Bible. His Collège de France courses defended the continuity of cultural and intellectual institutions; his was an "evolutionary" rather than a revolutionary philosophy of history. Michelet wrote on 2 May 1842 that God was not a destroyer but "the eternal artist." His theory reconciled the contradictions of Mother Death: the fact of mortality and his wish for ceaseless rebirths.

9 May 1842, Monday

Saturday and Sunday, I did not go out at all, because I suffered chest pains and nausea. I walked a lot in my garden and, whether I was walking or caring for Mme Dumesnil, I delved into my thought,

[29] Pierre Leroux (1797–1871), coeditor with J. Reynaud of the *Encyclopédie nouvelle,* published a confused but important book, *De l'humanité* (1840), in which he attempted to synthesize Buddhism, Pythagorean philosophy, and Saint-Simonism. Leroux was a socialist who, much like Michelet, sought to reconcile revolution and tradition.

I brought history to life, in the presence of destruction. It was living and it was dying...

All last week, since I had no courses at the Collège de France or at the château, I explored universal history for my benefit, and even before the advent of mankind, to understand how the mind was created, that is, how mind was conceived and given birth. That free creation will be next week's subject, for the final lesson.[30] This week, since Thursday (Ascension Day), I have explored the development from Abélard to the present, more specifically for my Collège de France lectures. My prevailing idea was that the modern era has been neither destructive nor negative. The Middle Ages was an era of war, and it dreamt of peace, an age of peace, like ours. It was tired of imitating and not being able to imitate, since the social conditions at the time were (. . .). Our modern society begins to fulfill the Christian spirit of peace.

My role as dreamer and nursemaid, during this beautiful and chilly month of May, among the faded lilacs, during the advancing year, was not without poetry. Harsh poetry in the presence of death!

Yesterday morning, Sunday, Mme Dumesnil was frightfully changed, emaciated, no more swelling in the face. Her eyes were huge and sparkling; with a feverish loquacity she expressed her satisfaction at having vomited fifteen times during the night. On the other hand, the two young people...[31] A frail future, and the past is lost.
Where is my life, where will I recover life and warmth in this impending coldness of old age and solitude? My life is where it always was, in what is always faithful to me, in history and the world of people. I return to it like Philoctetes to Lemnos, his island. Welcome me, beloved island, where I have spent so many years of solitude,

30 There were to be three more lectures: 12, 19, and 26 May.
31 Michelet notes that his daughter, Adèle, and Alfred Dumesnil were in love.

so many sweet and bitter years. Welcome me, welcome your wounded one![32]

The day before yesterday, Saturday, she was so exhausted that I continually watched to see if breath still moved her chest. Her chest would rise slowly, after long intervals. Her half-open eyes were sleeping, swimming, dying. The pupils followed the tilt of her swollen face: I have never seen anything more horrible.

In the midst of these emotions, I stubbornly excavated my thoughts. Which ones? Far too congruent with what I observed: the death and life of nations, the rough problem of destiny... This week something happened to me that I had experienced during the other; during the other, I had formulated the idea of a God-mother and of death as a childbirth.

Friday, research, scholarship; since Saturday, stimulation of the mind. Because I remained Saturday, I had a double day. That very day, at four o'clock, my heart awoke and breathed life into my subject; the Middle Ages was an age of war and dreamt of peace. Yesterday morning I recaptured the principle of war through Notre-Dame (the church of victory) as impulse of war. And at four o'clock, near her bed, I discovered something better, namely that the Middle Ages could not imitate because it did not sufficiently love.

10 May 1842, Tuesday

During these last two weeks, it was always the same routine. In the mornings, I would form and revise my formula. From four to six o'clock in the evening, I daydreamed at the foot of her bed, I penciled some notes, notes that often changed my whole approach to the question. For example, this Sunday, about the time of the

[32] An allusion to Sophocles' ***Philoctetes***. The hero was abandoned for ten years on the island of Lemnos. Michelet will return obsessively to this image, which represents history writing as a refuge. See below, entry of 5 August 1843.

terrible railroad accident, at the foot of her bed, I added this note: The Middle Ages could not love in a world of hatred.

Then, yesterday and today, the struggle became organized within my mind: between the Virgin and the Devil.

Dante dreamt of leaving on a ship for an eternal voyage with all the friends of his youth. Many times I have repeated that dream, with the friends I made through my teaching. My vessel was always dashed to pieces...

Apparently, the vessel must be the globe, and the friend must be humanity.

11 May 1842, Wednesday

The human mind does not change because of pride. The present era has less pride. The Middle Ages also needed to change.

12 May 1842, Thursday

At last I saw clearly, at my lecture, that I was quite right. At first, I felt it because of my deep serenity, because of my certainty. As I spoke it seemed as if I were swimming in light; I felt peaceful, humble and strong. Then, amidst the crowd, a quarter of which seemed to hold opposite views, I believed that I saw, little by little, a movement of universal sympathy. I had regained control... I noticed some faces: young people, serious and sad, who with each word looked at one another, a young lady with a child was taking notes, etc. During the lecture it seemed to me that Alfred looked better. Upon returning, I took a rather long walk in the rain.

Nothing happened this week. Sunday, I bought a calnia flower, which she gave to the nun for the month of Mary. Monday and Wednesday, I made brief appearances at the Archives because I wanted to return when the nun went to bed. A little hypocritical wheedling; she goes to the Jesuit mass. Bought a cactus at the flower market, not having found it at Silvain Péan's, which is located in the

Carmelites' very chapel, in their cemetery, where Mme de la Vallière was buried. Tuesday, I went to Neuilly.

13 May 1842, Friday

M. Lewes[33] for dinner, to whom I demonstrated, and perhaps excessively, the constant necessity for a faster productivity. Nothing more horrible: her delirium, throughout that visit and dinner. She sings and (. . .) out of despair.

14 May 1842, Saturday

Went to the Institut early, which I left at noon to see Giroux, M. Cellier, M. de Saint-Priest. When I returned, Dargaud, who asks me to write a memorandum on Cluny for tomorrow to justify his project.[34] Then I immediately read Lorain's *History of Cluny* and found that Cluny represented peace, God's peace, celebration, that is, the peace of the dead, stifled by the Cîteaux crusade.

15 May 1842, Sunday of Pentecost

Never did I possess less of the Holy Spirit. I undressed at two o'clock, expecting to replace the nun who was going to bed. Then, thinking better of it, I took the three children to the Trône gate, Bercy, the railway station, the Jardin des Plantes. From a distance, Vincennes, where the son and mother had lunched with the tiresome Monsieur C.:[35] That time was stolen from me. She herself had kept

---

33 George Henry Lewes (1817–78), husband of George Eliot, was a British essayist quite familiar with France. He translated Auguste Comte's *Philosophie positive* into English and wrote a *Life of Robespierre*.

34 Dargaud was seeking a government subsidy to research the history of Cluny, the medieval monastery. His employer, Alphonse de Lamartine, and Michelet wrote letters of recommendation.

35 Henri Cellier, formerly a lawyer in Rouen, editor of the newspaper *Le Législateur*, was a close friend of Mme Dumesnil's. Michelet discovered, after her death, that she had had an amorous liaison with him. Nevertheless, Cellier became an advisor to the historian on legal and financial matters.

me away, wanting no one. I slept badly, often hearing the nun, although she walked about barefoot. I got up at four-thirty.

Relationship stopped entirely. Two weeks ago, we could still care for her: cherries, grapes, strawberries, etc. A week ago, flowers. Today, even flowers were banished. Great restfulness, she is better. That resembles death.

16 May 1842, Monday

This morning she was more lively than ever: plans, a terrifying loquacity along with her so mortally altered face. Concerning Charles: "We must make a man of him. I will tell you my plans when the next school session begins." I found M. Filhos there; he was telling her about the Chinese war, the opium war. At noon I took all three of them to the Moscow Panorama display and returned home a little late (the nun had already gone to bed). Napoleon perished because of an act of faith. The Russians had such faith in their *father*, in their *czar*, that they never believed that he would burn down the city.

Upset more than ever, beset with ideas, with various desires, not even passions, I really need to summon my most fertile thoughts in this stagnation of illness in which, when the heart is dying, the body awakens. Oh, may that prolific impulse that produces man's tempests change into thought! May the ephemeral kind of reproduction become silent in the face of the reproduction of immortal things!

Yesterday, Sunday, Cluny for Dargaud. Therefore, I did nothing.

–Michelet relived Christ's death and transfiguration in the entry of 9 May 1842. He imitated Mme Dumesnil's ills unconsciously by suffering chest pains and nausea. He also indulged in odd pleasures. Although he found suffering repugnant, her slow demise inspired him: "Harsh poetry in the presence of death!" He translated his philosophy of history into a highly symbolic vision of immortality: Civilization marked the gestation and birth of the human mind. On Ascension Day (5 May) he defined its purpose: Modern society was the realization of "the Christian spirit of peace."

Another bereavement, as well, threatened him like another death. Michelet begrudged his daughter Adèle's recent independence. She and Alfred Dumesnil were openly affectionate with each other. By February they had agreed to marry, but, fearing the historian's jealousy, they had kept their plans secret. The young lovers' happiness during Mme Dumesnil's decline magnified Michelet's feelings of vulnerability. The elliptical flow of his sentences pointed to the hidden fears: "Yesterday morning, Sunday, Mme Dumesnil was frightfully changed, [. . .]. On the other hand, the two young people... A frail future, and the past is lost. Where is my life, where will I recover life and warmth in this impending coldness of old age and solitude?" The forty-three-year-old man, at the summit of his career, felt decrepit and abandoned! He faced a soon-to-be-empty nest. On 10 May a dream translated his internal combat into a prophetic epic. He became another Dante, steering a ship of humanity that was repeatedly dashed to pieces. The revolutionary orator, whose teaching was a "friendship" with the French nation, feared that he was an unfit captain. In fact, he admitted on 12 May that his lectures were a desperate attempt to regain control—of himself and of his public. Followers were required to steady his faith.

The religious calendar helped the historian to interpret his drama but did not lift him above it. He confessed his spiritual emptiness on Pentecost (15 May), the holiday that commemorates the Holy Spirit's descent upon Christ's disciples fifty days after the Resurrection. Their minds were inspired by tongues of fire, and they spoke strange languages.[36] Michelet, for his part, was an impotent apostle. Despite his charismatic lectures, he hardly tasted God's first fruits, and his sexual desires enslaved him to the body.

Michelet began to substitute a religion of the French Revolution for Christianity, but still another inner conflict delayed his conversion. He was a republican who ardently promoted the secularization of France envisioned in 1789, while his essentially religious personality—

[36] Acts of the Apostles 2: 2–4.

and nostalgia for the Catholicism of his youth inspired by Mme Fourcy—disposed him toward traditional devotion. How could he reconcile his yearning for faith with his condemnation of the Church as reactionary? He discovered a new source of revelation during Mme Dumesnil's final moments. Contemporary science demonstrated a spiritual presence within nature.

17 May 1842, Tuesday

My body was weak, my pulse uneven, I had chest pains, my mind was drifting. Rarely have I felt so low. I had died more than once, then died even to my death, that is, not consoled but sadly detached, whether by her harsh words and curtness, or by my preoccupation with work or man's mobility in situations that change little.

For the past two or three days, she was completely exhausted but serene. The day of Pentecost, she told Abbé Coeur that she was "with the angels." She was changing before our eyes, and she believed herself to be better. Her huge eyes stared. Horrible and sepulchral beauty. Especially in the evening, having asked that the curtains be drawn, that everything be opened, and staring at the greenery in the lovely evening light, full of plans and hope, she spoke words that broke my heart: "Aren't the woods still damp?" And again: "You will be very surprised when I ask you to do a thousand things." Moreover, nothing tender, except a word for Alfred. With all that, my heart returned to itself and became violently sick. I could not help telling Alfred how much I was suffering.

In the morning, after having written little and badly, I began to read Serre's article "organogenesis" in the *Encyclopédie*,[37] which M. Dussieux spoke to me about the day before. I had been overwhelmed by the grandeur of a science revealed to me all at once but

[37] *Organogénie* (on the development of fetal organs) was written by Antoine Serres (1786–1868), head doctor of the Pitié hospital in Paris since 1822 and professor of anatomy and natural history at the Museum. Michelet attended his lectures on anatomy and maintained close intellectual contact with him.

also deeply stirred by the determinism of sexual reproduction, by its influence on our freedom, on the destiny of free beings. Alas! Reproduction so often takes place without love!

All day she stayed in the middle of the bedroom, on the trestle bed; her face, hidden from the light, was even more funereal. Abbé Coeur was struck by it. That evening I found a piece of a note on the floor, which made me understand the nun's absence the preceding day, her clumsy little lie: going to get a night bonnet, etc. That is how everything intermingles, the lofty and the trivial.

18 May 1842, Wednesday

I defined the first part of my lecture: the maternity of Providence. There remained the objection: death. I considered it as a childbirth, as I did in 1838, when I had considered death to be the only way barbarian races could be educated. While digging into that subject with Alfred, something came to me, the idea that the soul, far from dissolving into some generality, must, according to our view of the ascending chain of beings, become increasingly individualized.

Ravaisson's visit.

19 May 1842, Thursday

I gave my lecture today, more people than last Thursday. No one I knew, except Mme Aupépin.[38] It is a new public that comes. In vain I waited at the exit for Pelletan[39] and Couture.

When I returned home, I found her facing the rue d'Ulm. She seemed less livid in full daylight but so feeble that she was not even able to suck meat. She appeared pleasant, happy to see daylight. Her

38 The family doctor's wife starts to entice Michelet by attending his lectures.

39 Eugène Pelletan (1813–84), one of the leading republican journalists of Michelet's time, began his career in 1837 by writing for *La France littéraire*. He tutored George Sand's son Maurice and became her private secretary. In 1842, Lamartine, following Michelet's recommendation, made Pelletan editor-in-chief of *Le Bien public*.

mouth was quite active and expressive, but her eyes were huge and staring. Yesterday and today she spent the day on the trestle bed, in the middle of the room, her face turned toward the door.

I felt pains in my stomach and in my chest, but I was determined to fight still again for my life, to renew myself, if necessary, with air, business, languages, countries.

Lanourais visited, to discuss the trip to Germany; he insisted on Swabia, as being the true German source, homeland of Schelling and Hegel. J. Quicherat visits.

20 May 1842, Friday

The result of my lecture was confirmed by the letter from the Italian Massari: "Yes, you have demonstrated that death does not exist."

21 May 1842, Saturday

I am going to see Quinet and from there, order some donkey's milk for Alfred.[40] Faucher[41] also recommends Dr. Broccieri's remedy. Quinet believes, which I do not, that Strauss[42] is from Swabia.

In the evening, Alfred told me that, since his grandfather and mother were dying, there were a thousand things concerning Vascoeuil about which he could no longer speak to anyone. Silence forced upon memories.

22 May 1842, Sunday

Visit from a discouraged Faucher, betrayed by his superior, O.B., happy with his wife. However, he sometimes notices that he married a foreigner. Then, the reading for the day of the Blessed Sacrament: *Quantum potes, tantum aude* [Dare as much as you can], which goes

40 A common natural medicine.

41 Léon Faucher (1804–54) was an archeologist and translator from Greek who became a journalist during the July Monarchy.

42 David Friedrich Strauss (1808–74) wrote the famous *Life of Jesus*, which boldly interpreted the Gospels as myth. Strauss was in fact from Württemberg.

quite well with my two present lectures. M. Lewes visits, very happy about Berlin, unhappy about Vienna and the South of Germany —on account of his adventures with the police? Walked for a while in the Jardin des Plantes with Alfred, Adèle, and Charles, who will soon retire.

I sat up with her for an hour or two. Not a word, as the doctor had ordered. She watched the street from the trestle bed. Once, as I lifted her up, attentively she examined the unpleasant night. She got up halfway and said to the nun: "I want to leave with you." And she remained thus for three-quarters of an hour.

23 May 1842, Monday

This morning, she asked for Charles: "Won't I see him anymore? You know how much a mother *would have* helped them." Tears came to her eyes and to mine. And she added, composing herself: "...*will* help them."

Friday, bought a window box, today a mantlepiece.

24 May 1842, Tuesday

Yesterday, continuous daydreaming, more and more focused. One begins with a brain, and one finishes there. That dreaming seemed to be an interlude between two lives. Today, lucid delirium, for she was conscious of the delirium.

She had asked for Charles, to give him her book; then she refused to see him: "We must protect him from such sights." She was extremely afraid of falling into torpor. She wanted her arms rubbed; she sheltered her two poor little thin hands in my sleeves. Ah! I would gladly give her my heat and my flesh. Her pulse was strange, lively and strong for such a condition. Her face changed often, often toward kindness and grace. At those times it was excruciating...

That instinct of dying nature that takes shelter near warmth and life makes me believe that the heart recovers. I believed it with passion, I fiercely pursued that idea. I soon had good reason to notice that the recovery, if there was one, was feeble, slightly affectionate.

She wanted at any price to remain awake. I did what I could, unaware that she had been given some morphine. I rubbed her hands, I warmed them for her. I spoke kind words of friendship, which she answered with gentle ravings, bizarre and uncanny. She said: "What's odd is that I am the nun. My condition improves, and what I undergo harms Mme Dumesnil." It seemed that was how she tried to explain her fear of torpor.

She sent me away when the nun returned. She was a little more alert. She took the small medal of the month of Mary which she had given me to keep. She pointed to the Virgin and the crucifix in her bedroom: "Here are our saviors. You need not display them, but keep them." She said again: "From the looks of the light, I think it is six o'clock in the evening." It was six in the morning.

Dinner between two sick people: Ravaisson, Alfred.

–Two weeks before Mme Dumesnil's death, Michelet, whose emotional needs were colliding, withdrew from the woman, while at the same time he lamented the numbness of his compassion: "I had died more than once, then died even to my death, that is, not consoled but sadly detached." He deplored the apathy that insulated him. We recall how shocked he had been at little Charles's "coldness" when his mother, Pauline, died in July 1839. Now, Mme Dumesnil's inaccessibility tormented him more than his own. Much of the time she was drugged with the morphine meant to numb her pain and dismayed at having to die. Michelet clinically observed the vicissitudes of her consciousness. Engrossed with her delirium, he commiserated with her suffering but blamed her for subverting their trust. Even the dying woman's son became a rival: "Nothing tender, except a word for Alfred. With all that, my heart returned to itself and became violently sick." Michelet was as starved for affection as he was tortured by Mme Dumesnil's martyrdom.

A grieving lover, he rhapsodized about death in order to console his loneliness. He savored the sadness of Mme Dumesnil's chamber, "especially in the evening, [after] the curtains [were] drawn." Outside, his beautiful Parisian garden, inside, the expiring woman's serenity electrified his imagination. He admitted that these pleasures were morbid, yet he reaped a full harvest of sorrow. This is not the first time we ask: Why such a voluptuous bereavement?

Michelet dramatized his anguish in an effort to tame his death anxiety. Writing allowed him, at least for solitary moments, to control the uncontrollable. As his own life seemed to slip away, he mustered his most intense emotions. No matter if they were melodious, harsh, or ambivalent. Michelet counteracted depression by swimming around in feelings. But the process was paradoxical: The bereaved writer amplified his misery in order to overcome the apathy that detached him. Literature benefited from this conflict as mourning rehearsed the artist historian's empathy. He identified with Mme Dumesnil's suffering while achieving esthetic distance through self-examination. Michelet's poetry of bereavement, like Wordsworth's, was "emotion recollected in tranquility."[43]

Natural science might resolve his religious dilemma. The historian studied his friend's article on the development of fetal organs and, with delight and wonder, contemplated the "evolution," within the womb, of the embryo to a full-fledged little person. This medical model reinforced Michelet's non-Christian theology of "the maternity of Providence." He became a sort of metaphysical gynecologist who envisioned death as "a childbirth." Science and philosophy appeared to confirm his fantasy of a female God.

Amidst these frantic speculations, Michelet still responded to people who needed him: Alfred, who was about to lose his grandfather in addition to his mother, and Faucher, who was unhappy with his job and uncertain about his wife. He loyally encouraged Mme Dumesnil to remain awake and conscious, but her morphine therapy made the communication he needed so badly almost impossible: "I spoke kind words of friendship, which she answered with gentle ravings, bizarre and uncanny." His jealousy of her Christian helpers shows that, until the very end, he sought to wrest her from the Church. The dying woman should ratify his worth and that of his personal religion.

---

[43] William Wordsworth's preface to *Lyrical Ballads* (1800).

26 May 1842, Thursday

When I returned, tired from my lecture, I found the cruelest sight: a jolly delirium, noisy and violent, songs, sarcastic remarks, all the bad aspects of her character were displayed, modesty ignored... I was brokenhearted. I experienced a moment of terror: She constantly stuck out her tongue. I was afraid she was having convulsions. Seeing all that in such a proper and reasonable person was the height of affliction. Fortunately, she quieted down a bit and was less boisterous when the bed was turned toward the window.

M. Lewes and Couture came for dinner. Rather late in the evening, M. Chatron arrived. I dressed again and took him to Alfred's house.[44] He does not want Alfred to travel at night and suggests that he spend the winter in Italy (Pisa or Rome?).

* * *

28 May 1842, Saturday

Weariness, weariness, weariness! But energizing, fertile. This season, so favorable to vegetables, our friends and nutrients, is an interlude for us. So much the more of an interlude and standstill that, after such a violent disturbance, after a two-year period of excessive production, after this last effort to regain control and to gather myself together through my teaching, my drive stopped of its own accord or only slightly oscillated. That is noticeable in my course itself. The motion, at first violent and painful, completely inspired by death, becomes more vital, pacifying itself, calming itself, diminishing.

Abandoned, left more than leaving, feeling myself all alone, turned back to individuality through Alfred's grief, I had him sleep near his mother, in my room and in my bed.

Today we were discussing the pleasures of the life to come, or rather we were establishing the certainty that all the analogies between present and past indicate future progress. To which he objected:

---

44 The doctor visits Alfred, who suffers physical reactions to his mother's dying.

> Yes, it's only a divorce, but for how long? And during that time of separation, we will have led a different life, taken on different habits. We will no longer be the same people!

I answered:

> Our progress will certainly be on two fronts. On the one hand, we will be higher on the scale of beings, that is, more individualized, but, at the same time, more interpretive and assimilatory. That is, as we become more aware of all the differences, we will also realize that they are generally exterior. The more we understand life's depths, the more we discover resemblances. Differences are skin-deep. The interior organization is quite analogous, etc.

(See in my lecture of January 1840 [?], the passage on Leibniz.)

29 May 1842, Sunday of Corpus Christi
M. Chatron advised us to take a short trip while preparations were being made for the long one. That brought the visit to Rouen up for discussion again. Alfred was deeply concerned about his father. He said: "After all, he is the only one in the world I still have." I accepted what he said, and I did not contradict him.

Weather was magnificent. No one visited. I read Geoffroy Saint-Hilaire at her bedside.[45]

FUNEREAL INSPIRATION

– Michelet will produce his most energetic poetry the following day, right before Mme Dumesnil expired. His rhythmic prose transcended

---

45 France's leading living naturalist, Etienne Geoffroy Saint-Hilaire (1772–1844), had been a close friend of Michelet's since 1830. The historian was deeply impressed—as was Goethe—with Geoffroy's famous 1830 debate with Georges Cuvier that prefigured modern evolution theory. Michelet began a serious scientific correspondence with Etienne's son, Isidore Geoffroy Saint-Hilaire (1805–61), in 1841 during Mme Dumesnil's demise.

grief as the writer, another Beethoven, captured the symphony within him. Michelet's philosophical quest will also benefit from the "sad and sweet" atmosphere. Two days before her death, Sunday of Corpus Christi, he will discover an alternative to the biblical Psalms that could not console him when Pauline died. Biology would now prove that the physical and spiritual worlds were essentially one; two important encyclopedia articles, and conversations with Serres and Geoffroy Saint-Hilaire confirmed his hope. In particular, the latter's theory of the "unity of form and of composition" reinforced Michelet's image of the animal world as one vast family.

30 May 1842, Monday

Never was my inner lyre more developed, more diversified, although, above all the sounds, a sort of fatigue and weariness muted them. The concert was vast and low, like five hundred instruments speaking softly...

Physically, I was very tired, not very sick. Two days of rest and donkey's milk had nearly made my chest well again. I was sorry to interrupt my teaching, to leave so soon the few attentive faces that floated before my eyes. The season was magnificent. Mme Dumesnil's health held us in a sort of captivity, sad and sweet. We took turns being with her. She was not suffering at all, her delirium had lost all its violence. But it was painful for her to breathe; we suffered to see her poor lungs gasp.

In the midst of this dying, slow and without horror, I persisted in seeking new causes of life. Hugo's *The Rhine* and Michiels's book[46] did not detain me for long. I probed and excavated the source of all life, nature. I read the articles *Animal* and *Cétacés* [Whales].[47]

46 Victor Hugo published a book of letters from Germany, *Le Rhin*, in January 1842. Alfred Michiels (1813–92) was a traveler who wrote for several liberal newspapers. He became librarian at the Ecole des beaux arts. Michelet was probably reading his book on Germany (1839).

47 Michelet consulted these articles in the *Encyclopédie nouvelle;* cf. entry of 24 July 1839 and note 12 (chap. 2).

The latter touched me deeply. A poem should be written about those poor creatures, generally sweet and intelligent, judging from their brains and their family habits, but condemned by the contradiction of their physical organization.

Saturday, I sent for Serres and Geoffroy Saint-Hilaire, who were at the Institut. I marveled how Geoffroy's bold mind refuses to acknowledge the genus of reptiles, classifying them partly among the fish, partly among the birds. The common people of Provence call the grass snake a "bush eel." The anatomy of the tortoise has justified M. de Blainville[48] calling it ornithoid [birdlike].

See also Geoffroy's odd note on the larynx of a street cryer.

Geoffroy first produced this genius for revealing life, which he has displayed in scientific work, in a heroic act. Unlike so many others, he was not able to abstract life from living beings; he could not, during the Terror, resign himself (as did Condillac's disciple Garat,[49] etc.) to allowing those he loved to die. His genius for life made him see a single principle in physical organisms. But by his very excesses, and by his incapacity to make distinctions, he views all life as beautiful, that is, he does not possess a concept of beauty: order and difference. To him a fish seems as beautiful as a man. Monsters captivate him.

He reminds me of one of those primitive barbarians who had so much life and blood in them that when they were killed, they continued to battle on. He reminds me of a barbarian who, without ceasing to be one, has invaded modern science, breaking down all our classifications as if they were useless threads. At the same time this strong and naïve man, this still childlike man (Ampère only appeared

---

48 The naturalist Henri-Marie de Blainville (1777–1850).

49 The writer and journalist Dominique-Joseph Garat (c. 1750–1832) was a deputy to the Estates General in 1789, minister of justice under the National Convention, and a senator during the Empire. He was an *idéologue*, disciple of Etienne de Condillac (1715–80), a student of Locke who traced the origin of ideas to physical sensations.

to be a child and because he was absentminded),[50] would constantly make people laugh because of his clumsy strength: Samson playing before the Philistines. Don't laugh. This clumsy child's hand can grasp and play with your columns, smash your temple, and without being crushed.

[Madame Dumesnil died on 31 May 1842.]

2 June 1842, Thursday
Everything is over. Alfred left with Charles, while I return from the cemetery, where I placed in the earth dug up from yesterday one pitiful little rose which, also alone, must languish and die there.

One year... so many things can happen in a year, so many events and emotions! One year to cross three worlds: cruel drama, of a cruel unity. I return to you, beloved other.[51] Welcome me back, as I am, and may I recover, if possible, my sad pleasures of solitude. "I was born alone, thus I must act as if I were alone" (Pascal).[52] It would have been necessary to act... But what do I bring back to my solitude? Is there anything left of me?

Monday, the painful agony of death. She complained from time to time: "Oh! Monsieur, wait..." Obviously, she believed that her pain came from a surgical procedure. I listened with terror, at the foot of the bed. Alfred and my daughter also. The doctor had reassured Alfred by convincing him that she was not suffering. That morning they tried to calm her with a little morphine.

I feel that in telling this sad story I am diminished. Words do

50 André-Marie Ampère (1775–1836) was notorious for his absentmindedness. He was a mathematician and physicist who made important discoveries in electrodynamics. Michelet was his neighbor, for his laboratory was on the rue des Fossés-Saint-Victor.

51 History, Michelet's "second wife."

52 Pascal, *Pensées*, no. 211: "We are fools to depend upon the society of our fellowmen. Wretched as we are, powerless as we are, they will not aid us; we shall die alone. We should therefore act as if we were alone" (Trotter translation).

not come to me, not even tears. I am in a state of extraordinary weakness and aridity. Can death be anything else?

Tuesday, her completely glassy eyes adequately suggested impending death. Sister Saint-Jules believed that it was time to give the last rites. Near the end of the prayers, at the very moment when they were burning the ceremonial cotton, with all of us present, she expired... Alfred fell to his knees. As my daughter wept, the old priest asked, "Is she her sister?"

I quickly sent a message to the painter's house and, while waiting, to M. Toullion's.[53] Both worked until eleven o'clock. M. Couture went to bed and made two more sketches the next morning. I wrote to M. Dargaud. Alfred was kept busy. As for me, most of the time I stayed with the painters, interpreting for them that sad and mysterious object. She had changed a great deal, suddenly, when she died. But from then on she remained the same. Full face, considerable nobility and style; from a three-quarter view, rather common; her profile, austerely graceful and almost ironic. Her thinness ennobled the lines. The only excessively large part of her face, the tip of her nose, began to disappear, began to reveal the hidden elegance of the person, in the delicacy of the bone structure.

In the evening, Alfred, a bit calmer, informed me just as Quinet and his wife arrived (Dargaud at Fontainebleau!), Alfred, I was saying, informed me of his mother's final requests: She left me everything, in fact, everything that the poor woman was able to arrange. Then I cruelly felt, and more still since our bitter argument of 22 April, what we were for each other. Of her person, she left me all that could remain, her hair. She left me that fatal ring that had cost her so dearly, with our own ring, the iron ring that she wore recently. Finally, she left her furniture, the cloths, which she had woven at my

53 Tony Toullion, a lithographer and portraitist, student of Amaury-Duval, who had probably done Pauline's death portrait in 1839. See above, entry of 25 July 1839 and note 15 (chap. 2).

lectures, as she reflected on my lessons (for example, those three days when she remained all alone), the cloths that she had begun at my home, for me.

Oh! It is indeed I who am dead, I feel it and I will feel it. Where am I myself, in this widowed and empty house? I am searching for myself, but I am no longer here.

Saw her room this morning: cotton and flour, the painter's bread on the night table, crucifix on the washstand, the pretty black bonnet, the red cushions, some oil, a letter in which she tells M. Renard about my lecture on barbarian law, about some papers I gave her in June for various uses.

Today, Collège de France, Archives. Fever, solitude.

3 June 1842, Friday
Paid Caroline.[54]

4 June 1842, Saturday
I went, with Boivin and my daughter, to deliver the death mask at Couture's house. From there to the Père-Lachaise to order a fence. On my return, Alfred's alarming letter. I arranged to book our seats on the coach. Never have I more cruelly felt such claws in my heart, pain by excruciating gashes...

In the morning, I had sorted out a few of their papers and found (dated 8 December 1837) a receipt from M. Cellier in the event of his death. [. . .]

–Etienne Geoffroy Saint-Hilaire reinforced Michelet's own prophetic defense of a universal life principle. Geoffroy proved his moral credentials by opposing the Terror that followed the 1789 Revolution: He had saved his friends from the guillotine, unlike the materialist

---

54 The Michelet family housekeeper.

Garat, disciple of Condillac. Geoffroy's scientific and moral life thus validated the historian's spiritualistic vision. Michelet, too, was "strong and naïve [. . .] childlike" and would prevail through his immortal writings.

Madame Dumesnil's funeral engulfed Michelet and he did not describe her burial at the Père-Lachaise cemetery. Rather, his heart went out to the "one pitiful little rose"—a symbol of their mortality—he had placed on her fresh grave. He elaborated the details of her passing and yet, surprisingly, this writing rendered him lifeless: "I feel that in telling this sad story I am diminished. Words do not come to me, not even tears. I am in a state of extraordinary weakness and aridity." Then he began to recover as he pondered his final memories. He placed himself among the witnesses: his daughter (Charles was absent), Alfred Dumesnil, an old priest, and a nun aptly named Sister Saint-Jules.[55]

As soon as Mme Dumesnil expired, Michelet challenged nothingness with art. He sent for two painters to help him "preserve death's tender graces." (Later, the bereaved would sketch her life story.) Poinsot and Pauline had shown that death could uncover the true person. Mme Dumesnil's flesh also melted away to uncover the ideal: "Her thinness ennobled the lines. The only excessively large part of her face, the tip of her nose, began to disappear, began to reveal the hidden elegance of the person, in the delicacy of the bone structure." We almost see Paul Poinsot's skeleton, exhumed in 1838.

Death also threw light on defects in their relationship. Michelet confessed his suspicions about his "white angel's" affections. He recalled the "bitter argument of 22 April" and, with acrimony, expressed ambivalence about their quasi marriage, symbolized by her iron ring. Mme Dumesnil's wedding band became "that fatal ring" that separated them as did her cancer. But the deceased saved the day. Her legacy of personal effects to him was a marvelous reminder of their authentic bond. She left him table cloths, concrete images of their intellectual communion, woven "as she reflected on [his] lessons." But

[55] The priest unwittingly points to Michelet's unconscious identification of the two Adèles when he asks: "Is she her sister?" The historian will suffer from his incestuous attachment when Adèle marries Alfred Dumesnil the following year.

what could rescue Michelet, who staggered toward the grave? "It is indeed I who am dead, I feel it and I will feel it. Where am I myself, in this widowed and empty house?"

Action extricated the survivor from his depression. Michelet administered his practical obligations: teaching, research at the Archives, paying his maid, ordering a fence for the gravesite, and delivering Mme Dumesnil's death mask to Couture. He helped Alfred manage his grief and studied the complicated will. The two men had to deal with the husband of the deceased, M. Dumesnil, with whom it was difficult to communicate. They all went by coach to the family's Sente-Bihorel, where they remained from 5 to 13 June. Then they quickly returned to Paris after completing their visits and financial and legal negotiations. The very next day they will pay their respects to Mme Dumesnil and Pauline at the Père-Lachaise.

13 June 1842, Monday

I said farewell. We left at four o'clock with Delaunay and Mme Teinturier. The sun was precisely behind the house of Sente-Bihorel, whose trees it illuminated. I looked back several times. Before leaving, I had sat for a while in the small salon, deserted forever more.

All day long I spoke about her with Alfred, each time more overwhelmed by my misfortune. He said quite justly: "She possessed, at once, a sense of balance and thoughts of the future, interpreting little." To which I added: "But she was someone we interpret." Poor soul who, with her wings, and wings of light, swam always in a swamp...

The businessmen were ruthless; they would have been less so had they intimate contact with her.

14 June 1842, Tuesday

Morning, at the Père-Lachaise with Alfred, my daughter, and Charles. The poor little rose of the day after is still there, dried and scorched. At my wife's grave we find the locksmith who is measuring our railing.

At two o'clock, at Neuilly, I gave a lesson on *the maternal govern-*

ment of Providence. The duchesse d'Orléans, knowing my misfortune, had come, as busy as she is with her three uncles who are in Paris.[56]

15 June 1842, Wednesday

As weak and feverish as I felt, I wrote six large pages about the life of Mme Dumesnil: her education by her brother.[57] Alfred had gone out to see the carriage maker; my daughter, Charles, and Marie to visit the Quinets. I returned early from the Archives, upset by the storm and by a thousand thoughts. I read several pages of *The Rhine* by Victor Hugo, which wearied me.

At dinner, Couture, to whom I explained the shortcomings of her portrait and my ideas about how he would paint her head with the velvet hat and the black veil... Alfred had given me her journal, and in it I felt all too strongly how intense the relationship between Monsieur C.[58] and Mme Dumesnil had been. I was upset, not so much by the thing itself but by the person's mediocrity, so unworthy of such a woman. At dinner, I was bitter, violent about human destiny, inspired.

In fact, it turns out that, of the three books of journals Alfred gave me, the first contains 1836–37, the second and third 1839. That means that 1838 is not there. 1838: their true crisis in Paris, financial difficulties, abandonment by Monsieur C., departure of Mlle Rivette. Early this morning I read several letters, which did not fill this gap for me.

---

56 Michelet had returned to the "château" to teach Princess Clémentine and her entourage. The duchesse d'Orléans was the wife of Louis-Philippe, the constitutional king of the "Bourgeois Monarchy."

57 Adèle Fantelin's mother had assigned the task of educating her to her brother Pierre, ten years her senior. She studied a little grammar, a little music, painting—up to a certain point. When her brother died young, she was married off.

58 While examining Mme Dumesnil's diaries, Michelet was humiliated to discover that she had had an affair with Henri Cellier; see above, note 35.

This is how I date that period. In 1839 Mme Dumesnil attends my course; vacation, she goes to Caen, Argentan; but not very satisfied. On 4 November she obtains a letter from Chéruel through M. Delzeuze, and sends me her son. In May 1840 she was deeply impressed by my course, alone in Paris and very lonely. She visits my house, and I go to hers. She consults me in June, just as I am leaving for Belgium; I suggest the Loire. She follows M. Renard and Mme C. to Switzerland.

16 June 1842, Thursday
Ran to Eichthal's, to the carriage maker's.[59]

18 June 1842, Saturday
Yesterday morning I escaped from my turmoil with great difficulty, writing farewell letters and examining my German files. During the course of the day, I made my little sermon to Caroline and Marie: to behave themselves.[60] To my daughter, another sermon: that familiarities devour... This morning, to the Père-Lachaise, and took back the rose of the day after, before the workers place the railing. The death mask, sent to the marble cutter, was delivered to M. Couture. Alfred leaves to consult Hahnemann,[61] and the post office. On the road, I chatted with Alfred about the Père-Lachaise: how it is not, as he had said, a meeting of indifferent people, how every man there is amidst his own, that is, amidst those who were men to the highest degree. As for me, I listen there to the lofty conversation

59 Alfred inspects the coach that is being prepared to take the family to Germany.
60 Marie and Caroline are the Michelet family servants. The historian will soon take Marie as his mistress.
61 The famous doctor Hahnemann, who treated Mme Dumesnil, now advises her son.

of Géricault, Parny, Bellini, Saint-Simon, Fourier, Laplace, Cuvier, Benjamin Constant, etc.[62]

[Trip to Germany from 19 June to 30 July 1842]

THE BATTLE OF BODY AND SPIRIT

–Love and work competed fiercely as the historian, stoically celibate, endeavored to hoard his women—the servants Caroline and Marie and daughter Adèle—and warned them "to behave," that is, not to get involved with men. His family excursion was another postponement. The German travel *Journal* recorded abundant meditations on historical method, intricate descriptions of visits, speculations on Oriental poetry and the afterlife, as well as a less spiritual curiosity. Michelet possessively endured his daughter's intimacy with Alfred. The young people had by then certainly announced their marriage plans.

The historian then surrendered to lust. When he returned to Paris, Michelet finally took Marie, the family cook, to bed, as the entry of 15 August 1842 suggested: "At night, during the hot night, I went to see her and admitted how agitated I was. This morning, however, after I woke up suddenly, I analyzed and bared my materialistic thoughts. I entered deeply into them but did not dare persist. The morning was ruined and work impossible. We went to the Père-Lachaise, where the flowers had been scorched." A family visit to the cemetery temporarily reestablished the self-control undermined by sexual tension.

---

62 See above, entries of 4 and 8 May 1834 and notes 39 and 48 (chap. 1). In addition: Théodore Géricault (1791–1824), who painted the *Raft of the Medusa* that now hangs in the Louvre. Vincenzo Bellini (1802–35), a celebrated composer of sentimental operas. Romantic utopianism is represented by Claude-Henri de Rouvroy, comte de Saint-Simon, or Henri de Saint-Simon (1760–1825), founder of the socialistic political movement that attempted to replace Christianity in the 1820s. Charles Fourier (1772–1837) founded the phalanstery movement, communes in which people were matched by their emotional character. Georges Cuvier (1769–1832) was the founder of modern paleontology and in 1830 debated against Geoffroy Saint-Hilaire's transformist theories.

In September he will "excavate" the foundation of his incestuous fantasies. First, by making Alfred admit he had found his mother attractive. On the 21st, both men, almost as father and son, will mutually confide their ambiguous attachments. The professor will take one step beyond, by pointing to the genesis of his bewitchment by death. He had always preferred older women (his mother, Mme Fourcy, and Pauline) or women the same age (Adèle Dumesnil, four months younger than himself). Michelet cherished these females all the more, in retrospect, because they were all lost. To retrieve Mme Dumesnil he prods Alfred and learns that his mother had felt more aroused by the historian than by anyone else.

Our selections resume as Michelet informs Alfred of his refusal to share his apartment with Alfred's father, "that bitter inheritance" of Mme Dumesnil.

14 September 1842, Wednesday

I told him everything this morning. Martinez[63] orders leeches for Charles. We go to M. Couture's house,[64] who sacrifices my second head and retains the first, taken in May, during the conversation with Dargaud. M. Cellier visits with his *Introduction à l'histoire comparée de la légende et de la littérature*. How could that cold, wrong-minded man share for such a long time the charming company that I scarcely had!

Mme Aupépin, beautiful and blooming, visits with her two children.[65]

17 September 1842, Saturday

Mme Dumesnil's portrait has been placed. M. Couture.

---

[63] A young doctor.

[64] Couture was preparing the historian's portrait, now conserved at the Musée Carnavalet in Paris; see above, entry of 30 January 1842, and note 11 (chap. 3). His more successful portrait of Mme Dumesnil now hangs in the Musée des beaux-arts of Rouen.

[65] The very day Michelet reproaches Henri Cellier, Mme Dumesnil's former lover, he appreciates the voluptuous Mme Aupépin's advances.

18 September 1842, Sunday

Martinez comes to examine me: long conversation about women, about his wife. In the evening, oily rubbing[66] (nothing since Sunday).

The entire week, Liège and Raes de Linthre.[67] I miss my daughter, everything has escaped me... Alfred suggests replacing Marie with his servant.

19 September 1842, Monday

The upholsterer comes to make the black cushion. It makes Alfred sick. Visited the Père-Lachaise with Alfred. M. Couture draws my hands, exaggerating them. M. Belloc[68] at lunch, recommends for Charles one of his professors, a careful man, good critic.

20 September 1842, Tuesday

Again Couture and his young assistant, who won an important architecture prize; he sketches the head. D'Eichthal comes to lunch Monday. At dinner, Monier, who had moved to Besançon: a true sphinx, moved, however, by memories of the Ecole.

21 September 1842, Wednesday

Yesterday and today I rather vividly captured Liège and Raes de Linthre. Impressed by my idea that total love can exist only between relatives. Alfred told me he had been very sensitive to his mother's physical charm. I too, remembering my mother, I have always loved women older than myself, or the same age. However, time and death

---

66 This probably alludes to sexual intercourse with Marie (in French, *frottement onctueux*).

67 Volume 6 (chap. 1) of the *History of France*, the story of Louis XI who captured Liège, with the help of the knight Raes de Linthre, and then entered Rouen on 7 February 1466.

68 A good friend of Michelet's, Jean-Hilaire Belloc (1786–1866), a student of Gros and Regnault, directed the school of design of the Ecole des beaux arts in Paris. He painted a charming, idealized portrait of Michelet in 1844–45.

cut such ties. Time weakens the elder's authority, and the young one necessarily wearies.

In the evening, music, memory, and flood of tears. Alfred contends that his mother experienced an excitement for me that she had not felt for anyone. Bold tyrant that she was then!

RELINQUISHING DAUGHTER AND MOTHER CHURCH (1842–1843)

–Michelet became conscious of his most primitive wishes during the year between Mme Adèle Dumesnil's death and Adèle Michelet's marriage. He worked feverishly on volume 6 of his *History of France*, but did not evade his obsession: return to the womb. He transcribed an incest dream on 30 September 1842 that echoed his yearning for both Adèles: "At night, I had the same dream of Caesar that I had two years ago.[69] It seemed that I told my mother about my privation of love. She answered: 'Well! Take this, my child.' I couldn't help relating this dream to people, but they just laughed and said: 'If it's the second time, you won't die of it.'" Michelet wanted his listeners to reassure him that his dream of intercourse with his mother was not a wish to die. He understood that his mother's vulva—only alluded to in the *Journal*—offered both shelter and destruction.

While he raged inwardly against losing his daughter, Michelet publicly relinquished his Catholic faith. He inaugurated a course in November 1842 that repudiated medieval Christendom. The following year, his lessons of April 1843 attacked the powerful ultramontane Jesuits, who threatened the autonomy of public education in France. More than a thousand students flocked to his courses and those of Edgar Quinet, with whom he joined forces. The friends became embroiled in a nationwide political battle. The government sent police and spies to their lectures while newspapers of various opinions printed polemical reports. Michelet and Quinet published their

---

69 See above, entry of 30 January 1842.

courses as a book, *The Jesuits,* on 20 July 1843. The authorities no longer supported the historian. On 23 July Michelet, on his own initiative, resigned as tutor to Princess Clémentine, to whom he had given lessons since 1830. Now an enemy of the Establishment, he embodied the French Revolution.

The day after he left the ruling family, Michelet yielded his daughter and revised his faith. The marriage of Alfred (age twenty-two) and Adèle (age nineteen) seemed to be another decisive death. The civil ceremony took place on 24 July and, surprisingly, a religious marriage the following week, barely three weeks before the historian's forty-fifth birthday. The day after the Christian wedding, he transformed his mourning into an ideological recommitment, as he bade a sad, though ambiguous farewell to his faith now past. With poetic eloquence he remembered his departed women and bravely faced the future.

[Adèle Michelet married Alfred Dumesnil on 24 July and 3 August 1843.]

5 August 1843, Saturday

Fide parum, tua serva et quae periere relinque [Have little trust, protect what you possess, and abandon what has perished]. That is the motto of old age, the reaction after great efforts. And the motto of youth, found in the beautiful reading: *Quantum potes, tantum aude!* [Dare as much as you can!].[70]

Returned yesterday and found my daughter's room empty!

Therefore, let us act, and begin as if for the first time. Now are you not young, very young? Is this not the dawn, springtime, and the *renascent season* (August !)? "Does the morning hour not give you the hope of plundering the lion's prey?" as Dante said.

Ah! So much has transpired, so many years and so many centuries

70 First cited in the entry of 22 May 1842.

have marched over my heart! There remains the *unconquerable will.*[71]

And it is this leonine genius that makes me unable willingly to resign myself, although the I that I surrender, I surrender it unto myself.

Farewell past, farewell sweet solitary years, farewell Adèle, farewell Pauline! All that is finished. As are my dreams of the Middle Ages. To me then, O future!

Unknown future, darkened East where so little light as yet appears! The dawn? Not even the dawn. If I anticipate the dawn, I do so in the chill of the night's last hours.

So I do not really know, as I feel this chill, if it is the cool breeze that announces dawn or the cold breath of the dying night. Is it the night that dies, or do I?

Because I, compared with better and wiser times, more luminous periods to come, I am the night, and I must make room for them. That is fair; let them come *dias in luminis oras!* [You pray for the days of light!]

Don't you see that Providence, in her stern solicitude for you, does all that she can to free you, to help you walk alone and tall?

The maternal care of a strict mother who, less anxious about her child's happiness than about his fame, brutally removes everything that might have slowed his progress.

Pauline? No. Adèle? No. The other Adèle taken from me as well.

And if you look toward the Church, if you sit in Saint-Ouen, I will take the Church away from you too. I will tarnish it so much with modern charms, roses, and worldly trinkets that you will have to seek the Church elsewhere.

I have already cut you off from Saint-Germain-des-Prés, which inaugurates the Middle Ages. Now I am going to take away Saint-Ouen, with which they end.[72] Lord, where then will I go?

---

71 English in Michelet's text.

72 The churches of Saint-Germain-des-Prés in Paris and Saint-Ouen in Rouen had recently been renovated in bad taste.

Go now, adore those stones, if you still can, defiled and modernized...

You considered Saint-Ouen majestic. Let's place a piano there, or some little drawing-room instrument.

You considered Saint-Germain venerable. Wait, we are going to turn it into a dress shop. The latest fashions displayed around the Merovingian columns, today's tastes amidst eternity!

The mason has found the priest, and the alliance of the two merchants completes the Church's ruin. The mason is a pious man, the priest is a pious man. The one will say to the other: You alone know Christian art, I will follow your orders. Do you want something pretty? I will make it; you'll see. Do you want something old? I will make it. Workers paid twenty *sous* a day will remake these cornices for you, each of which was an individual work of art, the intimate meditation of one man, as if it were a prayer in stone...

That's fine, my friends, liberate us from the past. Force us to press forward, to seek the future. The ravages of wind, rain, grass, moss, only increase our veneration. But what the rain and wind could not do in a thousand years, you will do, my friends.

Ardent workers for the future, who make a clean slate of the past, I salute you; to you goes the honor of having killed it forever.

Death is still life as long as the tomb lives as a tomb, through veneration, regrets, tears.

But alas! A pretty tomb, a stylish tomb, a tomb turned into a boutique, it is the death of death itself.

Still one more tear; and then, I follow you, O future.

In vain Vinet[73] writes in *Le Semeur*: "Is that what you are looking at?" Alas! It is not my fault if I placed the spirit in a body, if the better impulses of my heart were part of such a changing form: my mother, my wife, my daughter, and that great mother the Church, which I loved even more since I loved it with a free heart.

73 The Swiss theologian and literary historian Alexandre Vinet (1797–1847).

Farewell Church, farewell my mother and my daughter; "farewell sweet fountains which were so bitter to me!"[74] I leave all that I knew and loved for the unknown infinite, for the dark depths where, without yet knowing, I sense the new God of the future.

Ah! Whatever may be the one of your infinite forms in which you will manifest yourself tomorrow, I believe in you in advance and follow you.

As for those who do not need a living religion, who strongly fear lest we disturb corpses, lest we kill the dead, we will answer them that they, the half-dead, paralytics, the impotent, who do nothing for themselves, they should thank those who do everything for them. If they reap the benefit, so be it! And tomorrow let them become cabinet ministers, if they can, in the name of the causes they have combated.

One word, not for them but for sincere and unselfish people: When I saw that diseased thing, I was silent and I did not speak. When I saw it dying, I sympathized, I wept. Even dead, I would have respected it, would have sprinkled holy water. And if there remained only ashes, I would have held my breath so as not to scatter the ashes. But no ashes remained. [. . .]

–Michelet could glorify his role as prophet now that he had weaned himself from his Mother Church. A clever distinction allowed him to renounce his past even while preserving his inner continuity: "The I that I surrender, I surrender it unto myself." He could tolerate this uncertain transition—this "interlude"—because he believed in his autonomy, in his freedom of will. He identified with the common people who unified the nation, not with the aristocratic Church that divided. And yet his doubt persisted: "Is it the night that dies, or do I?" It was precisely that doubt, the antagonism between believer and skeptic, that fed his anxiety. How could he surrender his women and his Catholicism without relinquishing all faith? With bitter irony, the

[74] Another echo from Sophocles' *Philoctetes;* see above entry of 9 May 1842.

historian thanked those who had "modernized" the Church architecturally and trivialized it spiritually. That was worse than destruction.

The historian displayed the banner of "the new God of the future." He accepted the implacable march of time and cultural decadence while, at the same time, he embraced the cool dawn of tomorrow: "I believe in you in advance and follow you." Michelet trusted the unknown. During Mme Dumesnil's illness, he had postponed his break with the Church in deference to the dying woman. Now, after the "other Adèle's" marriage, he consummated the divorce. The week after the young people were united, Michelet, accompanied by his son, Charles, undertook research in Lyon and Switzerland from 9 August to 1 September 1843. His contact with the factories of Lyon confirmed his new political commitment.

INTERPRETER OF THE COMMON PEOPLE (1843–1845)

The *Journal* entries remained brief until Michelet traveled again, this time to the southwest of France (Provence and the Massif Central region) from 18 May to 22 June 1844. Action dominated his life. His notorious courses continued to provoke virulent opposition. He rushed to complete volume 6 of the *History of France,* which went on sale on 4 January 1844. During that period he also published an historical critique of Jesuit education and spiritual direction, *About Priests, Women, and the Family*. Remembering his subordination to Mme Dumesnil's priest, the author urged husbands to seize back their authority from their wives' confessors and directors of conscience. The book appeared on 15 January 1845, was immediately condemned by the Church and placed on the Index. Soon after, on 24 January, Michelet conceived the idea and the title of his germinal book of popular education, *The People*. His first historical volumes had traced the emergence of the common people in the Middle Ages from the peasant Jacques to Joan of Arc. Now he studied contemporary France's social classes and denounced their economic enslavement. The nation could be saved by a change of heart. Women, children, and the masses would show the way.

Michelet's intimate life was no less intense. By February or March

1844, he succumbed to Mme Aupépin, his physician's wife. He continued relations with Marie, but in November he separated from the cook and took the housekeeper Victoire as his mistress. To his mind she represented the dispossessed, and his duty was to educate her! He could not teach her to read, and the book he was writing became his only success. But Victoire satisfied his immediate needs. They maintained their liaison until he met his second wife-to-be, Athénaïs Mialaret, in 1848.

Another reverberation of Mme Dumesnil's death—the sale of her Sente-Bihorel estate—will finalize Michelet's ideological conversion. He accepted the validity of a socialistic division of property. The well-organized entry of 8 April 1845 will associate his loss of Adèle by marriage with that endured by Alfred, whom debts required to sell his mother's country home. Bereavement again forced Michelet to review and reinterpret his past. The historian renewed his sacrifice of Christianity and reinforced his identification with the poor.

8 April 1845, Tuesday

Sale of the Sente-Bihorel, Vascoeuil, on the sixth; Charles's dream comes true...[75]

On 9 August 1843, from the loss of my daughter I initiated an attempt to conquer the religious future. On 6 April 1845 I begin from the loss of Bihorel to seek the conquest of the political future. Still Saint-Ouen and the Sibyl![76]

A sacred history! That of the marriage of the farmer with the earth, the history of acquisition. In order to belong, the earth must be proportionate to the work of the family, therefore divided, whatever it may cost to see the property dismembered. Balzac in *The Peasants*[77] was not able to convey that truth.

---

[75] See entry of 19 December 1841, cited in the commentary at the beginning of this chapter.

[76] In pagan religion, a woman who predicts the future.

[77] Honoré de Balzac, in *Les Paysans* (1844), depicts crafty, dishonest inhabitants of the Morvan district in Burgundy.

In this sacred moment, when my family has just lost all ownership, when that beautiful estate, so full of my memories, escapes us forever, when even Vascoeuil,[78] Alfred's romantic fantasy, itself becomes threatened.

Witness of Mme Dumesnil's death, I hesitated being present at this second death, which, like the other, is mine, because the wood-paneled room where I shed so many tears during the first night (May 1841), because the wide path below on which I returned in the storm, having learned from M. Delzeuze that her life was condemned, because the little drawing room, animated by the invalid's chatter, the blinds, the view of the reservoir, and the doves at the windows; finally, Alfred's marriage, their bare nuptial chamber—everything deeply possessed me... Only Alfred's release from debts could counterbalance that attachment. The person, after all, is what personifies and enchants the place.

Sunday, 6 April, lodged for the first time at the inn in Rouen, I awaited the great vulture responsible for ripping apart the beautiful prey and distributing it. His calm face, typical of the Limousin, at first seemed vulgar to me, not confirming the model of harshness I had concocted. I went away, full of disgust for wealth and the wealthy... I was wrong. As I understood better, I realized that this man who does all that instinctively, without uneasiness or excitement (so it seems), is an agent of nature, like a chemical solvent that dissolves without love or hatred. He is a social necessity. We can compare the force of this legitimate necessity with the force of the hatred aroused by M. Dumesnil, who hindered us so stubbornly.

I relaxed, therefore, and on this mild April morning, imbued with resignation, faith, and vague hope, I walked around Saint-Ouen, below the beautiful church, in the monks' solemn garden. From there I heard High Mass; and the choir's voices were thus less discordant and

78 Vascoeuil, the other Dumesnil family property, was not sold. It has been restored and houses a Michelet museum and an art center.

seemed to be the voices of the common people... Outside of the Church and of the past, removed from property and present concerns, I was melancholy, but in God's sun I carried the future within me.

If I am not within that Church, it is because it has no future. If property escapes me, it is because the future wants it to be divided and proportioned to man's work in order to become more rightly possessed and more wedded.

–Michelet accepted harsh economic demands, compromised his ideal of private property, and in this way incorporated his family's *individual* loss into an optimistic vision of *general* progress. He managed to subsume radical discontinuity (i.e., loss of inherited possessions) into an overall, organic continuity (i.e., evolution toward a collective economy). This feat became possible by transmuting the lawyer in charge of "dismembering" the Sente-Bihorel estate from a messenger of death into a proxy of the life force. By a purely linguistic act he metamorphosed "the great vulture responsible for ripping apart the beautiful prey," a malicious extension of the obstinate M. Dumesnil, into "an agent of nature, like a chemical solvent that dissolves without love or hatred." Transcending his family's personal pain, Michelet absorbed Pauline, Mme Dumesnil, daughter Adèle, and now individual inheritance into a collective future harmony.

4 My Father's Death

JEAN-FRANÇOIS-FURCY MICHELET
c. 30 December 1769–18 November 1846

– My father has been my father, my origin and my *raison d'être,* in a more special sense than even that word expresses. I was engendered by his faith. Since my birth, irrationally and without motive, he had so naïve and so strong a faith in me that it gave me faith in myself. *Journal,* 21 November 1846 –

–Michelet became his own man at age forty-eight. His father, who championed his education and career, died at age seventy-six, abandoning his son at the height of his maturity. By 1846 the historian had identified fully with the revolutionary ideals so close to his father's heart. Before Furcy's death, his son anticipated France's upheavals and interrupted his *History of France* at the fifteenth century to construct two other literary monuments: *The People,* a book of popular education meant to convert antagonistic social classes to mutual understanding, respect, and love for one another; and a *History of the French Revolution,* which would endow Europe with a new secular religion. Two personal breakthroughs made these political expressions possible. Michelet organized his life story and finalized his break with the Church.

On 24 January 1846—exactly one year after conceiving its idea and title—he signed his magnificent preface to *The People.* This brief autobiography, which took the form of an eloquent letter to Edgar Quinet, described how the dreary First Empire, a period of mourning for the vanquished ideals of the Revolution, depressed the boy and made despair seem normal. Gloom was the canvas upon which he proudly traced his achievements, from his first job at age ten, *composing* (setting type) in his father's print shop, his initial academic successes, and the roots of his historical vocation. The author's history was exemplary for the common people. It was also a son's memorial to his father and to their shared faith in civilization. Michelet will draft it in his *Journal* on 23 August 1845, less than six months after the Dumesnil family lost its property.

23 August 1845, Saturday

I, my childhood, and the end of the Empire. *Dies irae, dies illa...* [Days of anger, that day...][1] Nothing did more to help me explain the grim monotony of the Middle Ages, the expectation without hope

1 From the Requiem Mass.

or desire, if not the desire for death, finally, man's easy self-surrender, than the fact of having languished, as a child, during the final years of the Empire. Today that period in which victories mark the years appears quite luminous. But then all was dark. France was dark; the light shone only on the army, outside of France, on such or other barbarian name. The principle of the Revolution, which had given impetus to those great wars, was completely forgotten. Most people did not know why they were fighting. Read the newspapers of the Revolution, which sparkle with ideas; amidst the rhetoric and declamation you feel yourself in the light. Then read the *Moniteur*, *Débats*, under the Empire. What aridity! What poverty! A book by M. de Jouy, an article by Geoffroy against Mme de Genlis, an ode by Baour, that typifies the entire life of the time.[2]

The spirit dried up, money dried up, the blood dried up. Every year three hundred thousand men left, never to return: the Minotaur's urn, but no more lottery, everyone was taken. Bloody death abroad, intellectual death at home, and no principle for which one would willingly sacrifice oneself. On the contrary, the press was attacked time

---

2 The *Gazette nationale* or *Moniteur universel*, founded in 1789 by the publisher Panckoucke, reproduced official documents from the legislature. Under Napoleon the *Moniteur* became a semiofficial organ of the government which was read aloud in the *lycées* during mealtimes. The *Journal des débats* was founded in 1789 and also reported discussions of the Assemblée nationale. The Bertin brothers bought the paper in 1799 and published important articles on literature and drama. Napoleon censored it, appointed an editor in 1807, and finally gave it over in 1811 to shareholders chosen by himself. The *Journal des débats* favored a constitutional monarchy by the end of the Restoration and was widely read by the middle classes and liberals during the July Monarchy.

Etienne de Jouy (1764–1846) wrote tragedies, comedies, vaudevilles, and a series of adventure stories. Julien-Louis Geoffroy (1743–1814) was a drama critic for the *Journal des débats* during the Empire and an enemy of Voltaire, whom Michelet admired. Stéphanie Félicité, comtesse de Genlis (1746–1830), one of the great ladies of the ancien régime, wrote sentimental novels after returning from exile in 1801. Napoleon paid her to write letters on literature, politics, and the arts. The classicist Geoffroy deplored the low literary quality of her romances. Marie-François Baour-Lormian (1770–1854), a lyric poet and author of tragedies, summarized the shortcomings of First Empire neoclassicism.

and again, and for the emperor's mistake, because he had reinstated the pope.[3] No hope. A host of people were profiting, following the army like vultures; and at home a small number of big businessmen, for whom protective quotas made it easy to hold us for ransom.

That period, which differed from the bad times of the Roman Empire and the Middle Ages by its glorification of the military, resembled them only too well by the contrast of tragedies abroad and futilities at home. Let us judge it by a small fact, pitiful to tell but very expressive. In the great troubles of 1813 and 1814, two things allowed us to survive: the sale of rebuses and of social games![4]

It must be said that no one took life seriously in those days. Everything that suggested a future, a rather long life, was neglected. What was the use? A man lived twenty years and no longer, it was a fixed limit. Life, why? Death, why? Who could tell? Miserable life, premature death, everything seemed the same. Why torture a child with painful studies, a child who would not live long? There was hardly any reason, it seems.

This idea and the particular circumstances in which my family found itself (sickness, anxieties) caused me to be abandoned to myself, without their sending me to school, of which I had a sort of instinctive horror. From the age of eight to twelve I remained without formal studies, without pastimes, without friends my age, seeing nothing of nature but the Jardin des Plantes, the edge of the water. No company other than my sick, worried mother, who did not even know where to find food for the next day. At that time we lived on a ground floor, cold and damp, on the rue des Saints-Pères. My soul was bare and empty, like the large, dark room in which we lived. Out of idleness

---

3 The *concordat* or alliance between First Consul Bonaparte and Pope Pius VII was promulgated in 1802. Roman Catholicism henceforth became the official religion of the majority of French people, and the Church acquired legal rights to property and education. Michelet's family was gradually ruined. In 1808 the father was imprisoned for debts.

4 Michelet's father printed rebuses and other word games such as Fabre d'Olivet's *Le Savant de société* [The Social Expert].

I used to read. My religious feelings were awakened by a book. As for me, I did not have the sun to worship: no sun at all in that gloomy house, or during the Empire's final years. At age fifteen I had heard about the sun. That was all. I knew that there was a sun for rich people, for the leisurely strollers who could leave those dismal hives called cities. Nevertheless, I said to myself: "It seems to me that God..."

The Imitation of Christ,[5] the hope of a world to come and where all this would end, a soft glimmer. Beyond that, I understood nothing. It was a comforting sweetness. But weariness might have overcome me and, if only I had known, a world of illusions. In my periods of daydreaming (1818, 1827, 1831), always thc same difficulties. Because of that I understood, later, how Christianity, having spoken for the people, had nonetheless acted against them.

What a dream were the Middle Ages, what a world of illusions, of daydreams! What indifference toward reality! The worker's indifference, for he does not work for himself: "Sow, sow, another will reap." Indifference of the Christian who hopes for nothing from this earth: "Above, above, here below nothing." What does he have to do with reality, with property, he who eats and digests his God every day and, within God, all that is? The God of the feudal lord, of the landowner, his Sacred Host, was his land, his fiefdom. That land is a feudal and a political person. In that living earth, he senses nature's life and its personality. The God of the nonlandowner, the one who owns no land, no fief, is the grain-God, flower of the earth. There he feels the life and personality of nature, changing life, spiritual personality. No involvement with the land. In vain is he enslaved to it, it is not close to his heart. He hardly likes it, that barren earth, which drinks his sweat and returns him nothing. He himself, mobile and floating, having no roots here below, is not serious about the flesh or about the

5 Michelet described the influence of *The Imitation of Christ* on his religious imagination in his preface to *The People* and in volume 5 (book 10) of the *History of France.*

spirit. He never laughs, he sings only during those horrible periods of dances of death, a true believer and ladies' man, eating God without result, throwing seed and love to the wind. The harvest did not arrive and the child did not live.

–This historical and autobiographical panorama explains the historian's religion of France. After the glory of 1789–90, the Revolution failed and the entire nation was bereft. Napoleon's foreign wars did not elevate France's domestic values and the young printer's son was convinced that life had no meaning and that his society had no guiding principle other than diversion or greed. The mature historian, after admiring Napoleon, never forgave the emperor for having rendered his family destitute. The Empire's demise in 1815 coincided with the death of Michelet's mother. Even before she perished, the busy child had felt imprisoned. Daydreaming and reading were his deliverance.

The boy's religion was otherworldly. His anguished need to believe in an afterlife emerged from reading *The Imitation of Christ.* No wonder Christianity maintained its grip so long after Michelet repudiated it: When confronted with emptiness or meaninglessness, he instinctively looked to the beyond. As a student Michelet "savagely" (as he said) isolated himself from classmates and restricted his social life. Independence meant effective work and many accomplishments; he recalled the important stages: loving Pauline (1818), translating Vico (1827), and proclaiming his philosophy in the *Introduction to Universal History* of 1831. Admiration for the Middle Ages motivated his first historical writings. Only later, after many deaths and disappointments, did Michelet imitate his father's disdain for the Church.

REVOLUTION OR NOSTALGIA? (1845–1846)

Furcy Michelet began to wane during his son's triumph. The prophet of the Collège de France continued to preach the Revolution that his father, and he himself, revered as the modern faith. He speeded publication of his ideological manifesto, *The People*, by having each chapter printed right after he wrote it. Michelet was still impassioned with natural science. In December 1845 he began to attend courses on human anatomy given at the Jardin des Plantes by Antoine Serres, whose article *Organogénie* had deeply impressed him during Mme Dumesnil's slow agony.[6] All aspects of his life were at full blast—carnal, intellectual, artistic. His complicated liaison with Mme Aupépin did not keep him away from his housekeeper, Victoire. *The People* went on sale on 28 January 1846, and his lectures continued to attract noisy crowds excited by his improvisations on the "French spirit" of 1789. From 24 August to 12 September he traveled in the north of France and Belgium to collect documentation for his *History of the French Revolution* that would erect a "holy altar" to his republican faith.

The *Journal* entries of 1846 are brief until 9 November when his father's impending death reawakened Michelet's need to scrutinize himself. The old man had been ill the previous year, but on 5 November he was stricken with lung congestion. Despite a momentary recovery, there was no hope that he would survive. The historian accepted his father's mortality without protest. And yet, again losing a beloved companion, he trembled for his fragile confidence. He doubted himself as an individual, as a teacher, and as a national prophet.

His father's burial will arouse Michelet's violent reactions against the Church. But he did not separate his personal grief from ideological perplexities. The son did not express his helplessness directly, nor did he seem aware of it. Like a timid child abandoned, he sought refuge in a youthful resource, his recently repudiated faith. Furcy had remained loyal to the Enlightenment, indifferent to the Church, while his son fostered a fitful ambivalence. Michelet will swing back and forth in the following entries: desperate, self-contradictory attempts to denounce Christianity once and for all while also preserving its spiritual substance, its ideals. He will then sketch his father's life story, hoping thus to fortify his own identity.

6 November 1846, Friday

My father indisposed, ill. M. Serres.

[6] See above, entry of 17 May 1842.

7 November 1846, Saturday
Course of M. Serres.

8 November 1846, Sunday
M. Serres. Visit to Mme Mickiewicz,[7] who told me about her cure; they wasted half the treatment.

9 November 1846, Monday
My faith! May it be granted to me, solid, and not die in me. For everything else dies.

My father, wrapped in Mme Dumesnil's cloak. And herself, I saw her die practically in Pauline's armchair. What do you want of me, O death?

And you, my fragile ones, Alfred, Adèle, even Charles, Etienne?[8] I feel like a bird precariously perched on a branch. My leaves are barely attached now. A gust of wind will come...

You then, late child of my studies, daughter of my autumn days, my faith, do not abandon me. If I could but establish you, replant you in the heart of the forgetful common people, I would doubtless gain my reward. But for me to be able, you must support me during the great human ordeals. The individual man must stand firm if you want him to support others. Become a support? When I feel myself flowing away like water?

18 November 1846, Wednesday
Returned from the Archives at two o'clock (reading of the regulations). My father...

---

7 Michelet had become close to Adam Mickiewicz (1798–1855), a messianic Polish poet who gave lectures on Slavic literature at the Collège de France from 1840. He was one of the triumvirate, with Michelet and Quinet, who inflamed the passions of revolution.

8 Adèle had given birth to a boy, Etienne, on 3 September 1845. His full name was Jules-Etienne-Félix Poullain-Dumesnil.

[Furcy Michelet died on 18 November 1846.]

19 November 1846, Thursday
Discussion with Adèle, Quinet. Will he go to the church? The young painter, M. Gilbert (rue Quincampoix).[9]

20 November 1846, Friday
Funeral. Two nuns come to ask if it is me. While going home I felt a sort of savage rage about that hideous burial...

The two nuns come during the display of the corpse and ask jokingly: "M. Michelet, isn't it?" Naïve hatred? Or, rather, were they ordered to attend, as penance? After my wife's death, Abbé Berteaud came running in the same way, trying to surprise us at our least rational moment.[10]

The same day, I receive two pamphlets (1829–37) dated 21 November 1846, one by Coëssin, the other by Charbonnel, a cured madman.[11] A few good ideas...

(*Five o'clock in the evening.*) Christianity has enslaved the human race. What did it do? It abandoned humanity to slavery. Some mellowing occurred during this reflection. Because of it? I don't understand it.

At first, the burial of slaves. The Church made free humanity descend to that level. It would have been better to elevate slaves to freedom. How does this differ from vanishing at the hands of a loved one, or being kissed by worms, becoming their plaything, eaten, devoured! Man perished because of man, by his hands, through human

---

9 As he did for Pauline and Mme Dumesnil, Michelet sends for a painter to immortalize the deceased. The "young painter" was probably Achille-Isidore Gilbert (1828–99), a student of Couture and Belloc.

10 Michelet will recall this incident in his 1869 preface to the *History of France*.

11 F.-G. Coëssin (1782–1843) founded a religious community in 1810 known as the *maison grise*. He made a celebrated pilgrimage to Jerusalem, which the young Michelet admired in his *Journal* on 26 June 1820. Jean-Baptiste Charbonnel published an *Histoire d'un fou* in 1837.

will: *Juvat ignibus atris inseruisse manus...* [He is pleased to have lent a hand to the funeral fire...].[12] You hand him over to nature. Because of fraternal feelings? No, you are enemies of nature. You despise the earth, you loathe what is green, you see a devil in the nightingale's song.

Neither heroism nor naturalism. What is your guiding idea? A bizarre asceticism that scarcely suits anyone, how much less my father, who was serenity itself. [The Church answers:] "—So much the better, we want to demolish it, that haughty nature, in order to improve it, to elevate it. We shatter the body and we save the soul." —Lofty promise! If you save mankind elsewhere, apparently you benefit it here below. Well then, show your results. The world was entrusted to you for fifteen hundred years. What have you done with it? You have conspired with Roman imperialism and the feudal system. What have you yourselves become? A government of Jesuits, allied with the government of king-bankers and banker-kings.

Religion of slaves, with what tyranny have you not collaborated? Religion of grace, of privilege, you have engendered, justified, glorified the government of grace,[13] that is, of favoritism and injustice.

Today, for example, how could I oppose your alliance? Was I free to give my father anything other than this hideous human burial, the only one permitted by the state?

My regret, I do not say my remorse—for I acted in good faith—is to have defined the ideal of those detestable Middle Ages. True ideal, such was its poetry, its aspiration, but what little relationship to reality!

I have stated this principle: "It will transform itself so that it may still live." Yes, it will transform itself but just as it transforms the dead who are entrusted to it. Passing through living destruction, it will continue in its substance but will perish in its form, in its name; more

12 Lucan, *Pharsalia*, book 2, lines 299–300.

13 That is, by the divine right of kings.

precisely, in its personality. When, having undergone that process; when, having been devoured by critical philosophy, digested by the all-powerful chemistry of the human mind, it will reach the state of humus, then we will be able to reconcile ourselves to it. Reconciled? Why? If it wishes to be only an historic fact, we will receive it among so many other historic facts. We will examine it with interest. We will collect its ashes, as Poussin[14] did when he was in Rome, taking a pinch of ashes and placing them in a traveler's hand: "Here, Monsieur, that is ancient Rome!"

We will also take a pinch of ashes: "Here, traveler, hold out your hand, make it hollow and small. Do you clearly see this bit of ashes? That was Christianity." Let us place it alongside the other extinct religions. It was doubtlessly one step, one era in the religious life. The barbarian elements it retained have made it disappear in turn.

I recall with distress the event that made me partial to Christianity. At the Taitbout meeting hall, I heard a very eloquent Saint-Simonian exclaim: "Crosses, fall from the temples!" It was the movement of 1831. I resisted, in the name of history. Then I said: Was another altar raised? No. Saint-Simonism is not an altar.[15]

But that No is not sufficient. If the defiled former altar, worm-eaten, forever prevents raising another altar, may the old one perish. What would happen if its close alliance with every tyranny should today turn God's altar into the devil's altar? No other altar has been raised. But we must raise one, a higher, truer altar. One which for fifteen centuries would not feast us with dreams like the one now crumbling, as it continues to speak of former miracles in order to hinder new ones, to prevent the simple progress of reason, of nature.

---

14 Nicolas Poussin (1594–1665), the great historical and landscape painter. Michelet cites a famous anecdote.

15 Michelet will recall this incident as well in his 1869 preface to the *History of France*. The Saint-Simonian Gustave d'Eichthal (1804–86) brought Michelet and Quinet to the Taitbout meeting hall where they heard Emile Barrault (1799–1869). Gustave's brother Adolphe, a banker, was also a friend.

My fine fellow, leave aside your miracles about which you have spoken at length. We don't ask you for the supernatural but rather to allow us to follow the even path of common sense. If the miraculous prevents the natural from occurring, prevents reason from acting, then, without further examination, we say with certainty: "The miracle is false."

21 November 1846, Saturday

Père-Lachaise cemetery. Sorted out my father's belongings.

And yet, these days, as I write this book,[16] while I forget the present, while I begin the Revolution again and I seize the Bastille, the great question of the present arrives to recapture me.

Here I am, near the bed of my already deceased father, ruminating dreadful problems. Will the world progress by translating Christianity, as I had at first believed, or rather by destroying it, as I believe today? Destroy? Let us agree on that word. Nothing is destroyed. Everything remains in substance, by means of transformation. But there are transformations that alter so completely... For example, the one that Christianity forces upon our dead, that cruel necessity to abandon our loved ones to the worms, the horror of feeding that hideous multitude. That is one of the harshest and most complete metamorphoses. Must Christianity itself thus undergo this ordeal, must it be devoured, absorbed, lose all its characteristic forms, subside into a state of inert substance and become cataloged in the great necrological museum where extinct religions sleep? Is that necessary, I say, for a new world to begin?

No one has resisted that idea more than I, no one has wished more for a gentle and regular transformation that would allow what remained innocent in the form to subsist. Error and weakness. The new life is more demanding: It requires sacrifice, the death of what pre-

16 Michelet was composing volume 1 of the *History of the French Revolution;* it went on sale 10 February 1847.

ceded it. The form implores in vain; none of its innocence remains when it obstructs the substance that will soon create another form.

—(*To my father, printer-bookseller from 1794 to 1812, born 1770,*[17] *died 1846.*) I did not leave him for forty-eight years, and I left him yesterday. I had to place in the ground him who loved only me. Today we are apart, he in the earth, where he has already received the cold November rain, me next to the fire, at the table where I write this. Harsh, bitter contrast!

Here I am, old today. "It is I who now," said Luther at a similar moment, "it is I who from now on am the old Luther." Old, debilitated, ailing, I take up the pen again, I return to my work, I return to my history, my customary refuge, the Lemnos of this Philoctetes: "Beloved cavern, gentle fountains, which were so bitter for me, receive your wounded one."[18]

The first day stuns, and we scarcely feel the blow. It sinks in during the following days. Memory returns, it delves into the wound, engraving it deeply, slowly, strongly, with all that we have lost.

My father has been my father, my origin and my *raison d'être*, in a more special sense than even that word expresses. I was engendered by his faith. Since my birth, irrationally and without motive, he had so naïve and so strong a faith in me that it gave me faith in myself. Undisciplined, I was given the most indulgent education, the weakest even, so that my father's faith in my destiny forced me to make it as he had imagined. It imposed upon me stubborn and implacable efforts, ardent and perseverant work which has not failed me for one day. I recover that work this very day as a refuge and a consolation, when I lose the person who was indirectly the cause of everything that I have been able to do. I say, indirectly. He himself never demanded any work from me. It never occurred to him that I had to

---

17 Jean-Furcy was baptized on 1 January 1770. I have given his birth date as c. 30 December 1769.

18 Another echo of Sophocles' play.

exert these efforts. He believed that I would attain everything by the strength of my nature. I did not see things in the same way. The less he demanded, the more I did.

He himself was the son of grace. He never really understood the man of work, which I was. My constant work, solitary and almost savage, kept me separated from him. I lived near him, with him, and yet saw him only briefly. I greatly regret that. I profited too little from those irretrievable days. With him so many things have perished, not only for the son but even for the historian. He had witnessed the ancien régime, the Revolution, the Empire, the Restoration with the July Revolution, and the ruin of July. He was tradition. This he was especially for the eighteenth century and for the Revolution. He was born eight years before the death of Voltaire; he was twenty years old in 1790. His best period was during the last years of the Republic, from '94 to '98. The year 1798, when I was born, saw the beginning of the weakening, the death of the press, the ruin of printing, annihilated under Napoleon. I can say that before 1800 my father begins to die within himself, to live through me, in his faith in my future.

He belonged essentially to the eighteenth century, to Voltaire's and Rousseau's century. His opinions or habits of thought were of that time, and he hardly ever deviated from them. An almost indifferent witness to what has happened since, he let the world flow by. The most horrible catastrophes, private and public, even his own ruin, did not at all shake his serenity. We were often surprised that it was so. We could not guess why. It is because he did not live within himself, not within the present but in the future, in me.

As for me, during my early years he watched me become restless, swim in the tide of time and opinions. Emerging from the eighteenth century, at times I would leave it for a moment, always to return. I always recovered my father, that is, the true France of Voltaire and Rousseau. My strange whims never troubled him. He viewed them with indulgence: The son in whom he had faith could not become estranged from him, since he carried him within himself.

That indulgence, that facile hope in my future wisdom shattered twice, in two circumstances that I must mention at the expense of my self-esteem. The first time, when I was eighteen years old, my heart softened by the age of love and imagination, I suffered from not belonging to the great Christian alliance, the only one, alas! which still exists (. . .).[19]

Yesterday, under a cold November rain, I put my father in the earth. The horror of the season added to the horror of his burial's frightful form. We tolerated it, as long as we could believe in the promises of Christianity. Now that it has had the world in its control for fifteen hundred years without doing anything for it, it is nothing but an obstacle. It is harsh, odious, to endure this burial as a slave. We accepted it while Christianity promised freedom. It did not give freedom. But, although it despised the body, it became material. It was always the ally of tyranny: the Empire, the feudal system, today the Bank.

My outrage at all this, aroused by the harsh and mercantile props of the funeral procession, gave me some strength. I left, aged by the death of my father, coughing, sickly. Outrage restored me, I returned on foot.

What did I do when I embellished the ideal of the Middle Ages? Did I hide reality? I worked against myself, against the progress of the world. How essential it is that I remain alive in order to weaken the deadly prejudices that I upheld, without being aware of it!

–Michelet's almost visionary *History of the French Revolution* meant to overthrow the "defiled former altar, worm-eaten," of Christianity, once cherished, and replace it with a nationalistic secular faith. The author's preface denounced the religion of grace, of fa-

[19] The manuscript unfortunately breaks off here. Michelet alludes to his baptism, on 23 June 1816, under the influence of Mme Fourcy. The second failing must be his Saint-Simonian temptation mentioned in the preceding entry (and note 15).

voritism and arbitrary privilege, in favor of the democratic principles of justice and equality. Was his conversion complete? Now that his father was no more, the historian stood at a crossroads: He could bring his anticlericalism to its logical conclusion by condemning the Church as irremediably pernicious, or he could do intellectual acrobatics so as to salvage the institution. Would he "destroy" Christianity completely or "translate" it? Michelet's words were precise. He resolved to "destroy" Christianity; but instead he "translated" it into another cultural form, whose model was the 1789 Revolution.

These oratorical reflections ebb and flow with a prophet's alternating regret and indignation. Michelet blamed the Church's distrust of nature and subversion of social equity while he sympathetically mourned its decadence. Unwittingly he bolstered his ambivalence. He saw the Church less as a political or community institution than as an organic entity with a life cycle of its own. On 20 November, the day he placed his father in the ground, Michelet formulated a subtle distinction: He separated the Church's spiritual substance (in French, *la matière*) from its historical reality (*la forme*), what he called its "personality." Michelet's technical terms were quite deliberate. He reasoned by analogy and elaborated metaphors—hardly a rational method! His verbal fantasy redefined the Church's immortal spirit, attempting thus to reconcile two mutually exclusive images: the Church as either humus (that is, decomposed vegetable matter, fertile soil) or inert ashes. Michelet maintained both views.

The next day he sorted out his father's belongings and put the finishing touches on his dramatic set piece, the capture of the Bastille.[20] He searched within himself, denied the death of his mother Church, and then redefined the word "destroy," taken so literally the previous day: "Nothing is destroyed. Everything remains in substance [like humus], by means of transformation. But there are transformations that alter so completely..." Michelet translated the word "death" into its opposite! Death became "one of the harshest and most com-

[20] The *French Revolution*, book 1, chap. 7. The author's preface of 1847 evokes his father's death: "When that happened, I looked, I was elsewhere, so I quickly began this work, which I had dreamt about for so long. I was at the foot of the Bastille, I was storming the fortress, I unfurled the immortal flag on its towers... The blow of his death came suddenly, like a bullet from the Bastille..."

plete metamorphoses." The artist had again conquered extinction. Death became a progressive evolution, a change from one life form to an advanced stage of being. Denial of death was Michelet's true agenda. If nature replaced the Christian God, something of the Church—in its spirit—would remain immortal. Nothing cherished should ever disappear altogether.

Furcy Michelet, too, lived within his son who incorporated his father's life story into his own. The loving memorial that began "*To my father, printer-bookseller from 1794 to 1812, born 1770, died 1846*" became an autobiography. Michelet justified his brutal work ethic—and the guilt it implied—as repayment for his father's unmotivated and selfless faith in his gifted son. (The historian's entire career might be considered as reparation for the extended family's self-sacrifice.) When his father died, he reproached himself for favoring his career, as he had when Poinsot and Pauline departed. At last, protected on the Lemnos that history writing represented, he clinically observed his grief: "Memory returns, it delves into the wound, engraving it deeply, slowly, strongly, with all that we have lost." What a lucid, poetic way to describe the introspection that follows bereavement.

Now alone, the sophisticated historian had to make the simple person's faith his own. The following day, the twenty-second, he will prepare himself by reformulating, once again, his condemnation of the Church. Returning immediately to the *Journal*, he abandons biological metaphors in favor of a direct ethical verdict.

22 November 1846, Sunday

Can dead Christianity be transformed? Christianity is dead in whatever it has that is Christian. It was the religion of grace; and now the question of grace is extinguished in every mind, killed by the advent of justice. Look at the Protestant countries, which alone adopted that doctrine, which is the very root of Christianity: They lean toward skepticism about the holy and about justice, about grace and about law, or rather they are petrified in methodism.

Christianity still lives only in its non-Christian elements, in the part that it borrowed from paganism, changing it a bit, in the worship of the Virgin and the Saints, in the materiality of the Sacred Heart. But it joins to this pagan, sensual aspect, which appeals to matter, the so-called spiritual aspect, the claim of knowing every thought, the inquisition of the confessional, less dangerous for morals, perhaps, when Christianity had not reached its pagan period.

Therefore, today, it is an inquisitorial paganism, assimilating the evil of both religions. It is perpetuated solely by its action on the weak and the disarmed; that is, it works by surprise. It seizes the woman, which results in the interior divorce of the family. It takes the child, which results in the impossibility of progress. And it does not keep the child, which results in disharmony within the whole of society, skepticism, and moral flippancy.

Here, every tyranny in the world is its helper. All want mankind to become discordant, therefore weak. They want us to accept the dogma of God's elect, God's elected powers, the legitimacy of privilege, in other words, the justice of injustice, the legality of illegality.

Can Christianity be transformed; that is, change from grace into justice and become equitable? Then salvation would be the just reward for deeds. Then it would not be the result of grace, of God's choosing. It would not be the consequence of Christ's sacrifice. Thus, Christianity would be useless. If Christianity sides with justice, there is no longer Christianity. When Christianity became a judge, through the Jesuits, etc., it flouted both law and grace.

Family discussion, Thursday, between the death and the funeral. Such an intimate shock forced me to reflect. The deceased man's opinion, which I knew so well, assured me that no display of worship, formal and exterior, would seem necessary. There remained another, very serious difficulty that my daughter brought up. The church is the meeting place, the only place where people pray together, bless together. Why deprive the deceased of that fraternal benediction?

Why? Because it is not fraternal benediction but the priest's, that which the priest derives from grace. And grace, what is it? Undeserved favor: "I have elected you always." Or, if it is deserved, it is by him who has believed: "*Qui crediderit in me*" [He who will have believed in me].[21] He who has believed? These days, I have not yet found him. There are enough people who believe that they believe, who affirm so as to convince themselves. Who can believe today that God saves according to favor, that salvation is an arbitrary and capricious privilege?

Whatever you think, people today believe with firm faith. The world believes in justice, in equal justice, without privilege; no more elected few. Have we thus returned to Papinian, to Caesar's justice? No, it is no longer the *praetorium* [court of justice], marked with martial toughness, which obtains equity only by trickery. It is no longer the *responsiones* [opinions] of erudite judges. It is a human justice, that is, always weighing human weaknesses and the determinism of nature (extenuating circumstances).

23 November 1846, Monday
Kept at home because of colic; very weak.

24 November 1846, Tuesday
Waited for M. Letronne at the Archives.

25 November 1846, Wednesday
Resumed work.

26, 27 November 1846, Thursday, Friday
Finished the capture of the Bastille. Père-Lachaise.

---

21 See the Magnificat of Pentecost. Michelet has paraphrased a quotation, concerning Christ's resurrection of Lazarus, carved on one portal of the Père-Lachaise: "*Qui credit in me, etiam si mortuus fuerit, vivet*" [He who believes in me, though he die, yet he shall live] (John 11: 25).

28 November 1846, Saturday
Gave the first permission to start printing my *History of the French Revolution.*

Yesterday, went to Quinet's and to the Père-Lachaise with Alfred.

A vast depth, of boundless melancholy, which floods over everything, but with so many exterior and interior reasons to recover. Gentle sadness, but vast. An endless fog, a gray ocean, which contains everything, even the most beloved, the most colorful things. And, everywhere, the fog still overflows.

The capture of the Bastille, my imminent lectures, the Quinet affair. Alfred, Adèle, Charles have been so wonderful for me...
Let us thank Providence and gently head toward the other land. I have already taken a huge step. I feel that I am moving forward.

THE PRIEST CONFESSES (1846–1847)

–Michelet did indeed "move forward" during the year after his father's death. Accomplishments seemed to tumble one upon the other in his calendar. Barely ten days after the burial, he completed the capture of the Bastille, the cornerstone of his *History of the French Revolution.* The next day, on 28 November 1846, he approved the first printer's proofs of volume 1. While volume 2 of the *Revolution* was well underway the first went on sale on 10 February 1847; the very next day, the author resumed his inflammatory Collège de France lectures, this time on "Mirabeau and the Spirit of the Revolution." On all fronts he challenged the powers that be. He was the priest of the new religion.

But Michelet felt destitute at the one-year anniversary of his father's death. Furcy had died on 18 November 1846, and continuous work did not fill the void. On 12 November 1847, a week before the anniversary, the historian corrected the proofs of volume 2 of the *Revolution,* in which he defined the book's "spirit and method." On the anniversary, he relived the experience of his father's death.

The following selections begin on the day volume 2 went on sale. Michelet will confess his impotence the following week, right after the anniversary. He will lucidly define his competing drives: (1) art, a lust for beauty, represented by Rembrandt; (2) political utopianism, embodied in the teaching of his colleague Adam Mickiewicz; and (3) the non-Christian reverence for life of the physiologist Antoine Serres. The central paradox of his moral life, first revealed during his mother's death, remained unchanged: the battle, within himself, between the egotistical "artist" and the socially responsible "historian," between "individuality" and "generality."

15 November 1847, Monday
Publication of volume 2 of the *History of the French Revolution.*

19 November 1847, Friday
Yesterday, the anniversary of my father's death. Rarely have I been more emotionally dejected. Tendency toward individuality; generality calls me, but I am at a dead end. Thus, during these twelve months, I have experienced a constant thrust toward the outside; and inside, I remain empty. Seek strength from art (Rembrandt), from humanity (Mickiewicz), from nature itself (Serres), from living, suffering nature: "Beg for a living near the poor."

Dreamt about the state of the world and how to serve it: by anticipating? by seeing what is to come? Search within myself, within life, in order to counterbalance the frightful indigestion of books that I have just endured.

I went to see Mickiewicz.

20 November 1847, Saturday
From the fourteenth to the twentieth, contraction and examination of self, a moment of moral reflection. On 14 November: *tà ektós* [exterior things]. On 19 November: *tà éntos* [interior things]. The influenza that seized me afterward prevented me from gaining renewed strength, as I had planned, through charitable visits, etc. Expansion took place (advice of clemency to Prussia and the Swiss) but without fortifying myself to the depths.

How am I not the true priest, I who this year celebrated the holy of holies on the altar of the Federations?[22] How can those sublime things, which drew tears from my eyes, remain so far from my intimate life? How does nature stubbornly return to make one descend to individuality? What is the path? Before formulating any idea, expand the heart, awaken the desire for brotherhood.

The artist's danger: pointed out profoundly by Dugald Stewart,[23] although indirect. Those who speak the most about virtue practice it the least. Hypocrisy? No, but they relieve with words the need that we all have for goodness. They no longer need to act.

(*At the Archives.*) Montesquieu speaks about an evening at the theater after which, he says, he made a firm resolution to live as a gentleman. I experienced that yesterday evening, a beautiful November evening: no more day, no more light. I returned from seeing Mickiewicz and, still excited, I felt a most intense compassion for mankind, with a little scorn and reproach for the selfish artist shut in his study, enjoying himself in his way. My heart was moved to the utmost depths. I grieved, I envied those manly qualities that alone allow true tenderness. My life did not prepare me for it. May God give it to me through His grace! To be an artist is to create. But to create, one must be.

Today, looking for clothing to give away this winter, my daughter offered her mother's dresses. Alas! They are ruined. If she were consulted, she would prefer that these wool clothes be used to warm God's poor creatures... At least I can keep a few of them. Let us give ourselves. But are we not allowed to save a memory? Sweet years

---

22 The second impressive set piece of the *Revolution* was Michelet's ecstatic description of the Feast of the Federations of 14 July 1790, the "new religion" (book 3, chap. 12). At that moment, according to the historian, France's diverse provinces reached a quasi-mystical state of unanimity.

23 Dugald Stewart (1753–1828) was a Scottish philosopher who deeply influenced Michelet in his youth. The first volume of his *Elements of the Philosophy of the Human Mind* was translated into French by Prévost in 1808.

of silence, of unrecognized work, of poverty, of abstinence, of a modest and faithful life, will you have perished in everything except in a corner of memory? And still, in this impassioned life in which days urge on the days, I spend entire years without returning to reflect upon myself, without a memory of myself, and scarcely one of you who loved me so and were mine.

To be more than to appear. To steep oneself in being. Absent from realities for so long, exiled in a world of paper, return, O my soul, my daughter, return to your beginnings. The day before yesterday, you passed very close to the rue de Périgueux, close to the place of your afflictions.[24] Experience, thus, the afflictions of mankind. Behold the winter and, as the pompous Frisian citizen says: "Live in everyone, share your soul, give of it to all people." And for you to do that, you must achieve a greater detachment. You have a limp and lazy soul. You enjoy the fireplace, the home, your sleep. You feel all that, when you return home in the evening, more than any man should (a man should know all too well that so many others lack it!). You still strongly feel, without protection, the lightning bolt of beauty. You must elevate yourself, in love, to greater heights, beyond sensuality.

On spiritual beggary: Beg for a living, next to the poor. You will become a man. You will be less of a book, less of a scribe, less of a legless cripple, less of a dreamer, less vain, less subtle. Perhaps, you will cure that artist's slackness, to which Dante so sadly confessed. You will be less sensitive to dreams, to women, that living dream. Your sensitivity will become strength and courage (to suffer with the world that suffers).

Remarkable strength of nature, wealth of poverty, health of suffering! It will give to each of us exactly what we lack. To the excitable

---

24 Michelet's family had moved to the rue de Périgueux at the end of 1813. His mother died there on 9 February 1815. Soon after, father and son moved to Dr. Duchemin's clinic on the rue de Buffon, where the young man met Mme Fourcy and then Pauline. See above, Prologue, note 7.

artist, strength and truth: life is not a sheet of paper, or an Oriental thought, or light fog, where a thought dances... To the suffering woman, it gives love. To the child, initiative. To the young man, a support through temptations, the continence that produces energy: continence is concentration. [. . .]

–"To be an artist is to create. But to create, one must be." How could Michelet preserve the freedom of his solitude, safeguard his inner universe, while actively caring for others? What was his true vocation? The death of each loved one renewed the questions. He cried out again one year after his father's death: "To be more than to appear. To steep oneself in being. Absent from realities so long, exiled in a world of paper, return, O my soul, my daughter, return to your beginnings." Solitude or solidarity? His momentous entry of 20 November 1847 defined the complete rhythm of his being. First, contract inward and examine yourself deeply; then, pour yourself outward, "expand the heart, awaken the desire for brotherhood." Self-absorption was the heart's systole, and compassion its diastolic flow. Could he reconcile them?

A family incident symbolized the conflict once and for all. When his daughter wanted to donate some of her mother's dresses to the poor, the historian automatically begrudged her charity, for Pauline's tattered garments were his memories, relics of their love. Should he preserve the past at the expense of the living? Could he as an artist, an intellectual, a writer "exiled in a world of paper," morally justify his withdrawal? Was it true that "Those who speak the most about virtue practice it the least" because "they relieve with words the need that we all have for goodness"?

The historian struggled to elevate self-concern to the level of selfless love. Systematically, he attempted to sublimate his hedonistic desires into practical acts. Writing his bereavement allowed him to immolate his sensual self and offer it upon the altar of generosity; writing required an artistic asceticism, what he called "spiritual beggary." He could not master death, but he could control his "prolific impulse," —or so he thought.

5 Exhumation and Reburial of My Father and My Son

YVES-JEAN-LAZARE MICHELET

2 July 1850–24 August 1850

– He was born to me the very year which completed the first half of the present century. I named him Lazarus in my devout hope to awaken the nations. I had imagined that I saw a gleam upon his face, as it were, of the strong and tender thoughts which throbbed in my heart during the final moments of my teaching. Oh vanity of human hopes! *The Insect* (1857) –

—Michelet's responses to the death of his infant son Lazarus appropriately conclude *Mother Death*. Mourning had cultivated a creative method. Bereavement forced him to reexamine himself, while mourning—the survivor's adjustment to loss—would animate knowledge and literary works. When Poinsot's departure from Paris called the *Journal* into being, Michelet's precocious autobiographical notes began to anticipate his mature vision. When Poinsot died, the survivor sought to resurrect the past, in the *Memorial* as in the *Journal*, and History emerged. We have thus followed the genesis of Michelet's vocation from his mother's death in 1815 to his father's in 1846. When she died, he preserved his Latin assignment as a memorial; his *History of the French Revolution* was a fitting shrine to his father. The symmetry of these selections is indeed fearful. *Mother Death* starts in 1815 and ends in 1850, right before Michelet's fifty-second birthday, as he buried his own son beside his own father.

SECOND MARRIAGE, SECOND LIFE (1846–1850)

Michelet's political prestige ended between his father's death and, four years later, his exhumation. The historian's Collège de France lectures, entitled "Social Renewal and Revolution," may have contributed to the 1848 insurrections. On 2 January 1848 Salvandy, the Minister of Education, suspended his course and those of Quinet and Mickiewicz. Michelet then published them weekly as pamphlets, while he advanced his *History of the French Revolution*. After the upheavals of 22–24 February, Michelet and Quinet victoriously returned before their cheering students, in the presence of Mickiewicz's empty chair, to proclaim the new Republic. But the violent repression of a workers' protest, from 23 to 26 June, halted all utopian hopes. The first half of Michelet's life, and that of the Romantic generation, was finished.

A new existence began when he fell madly in love with a woman he would worship until his death. On 8 November 1848, he first met twenty-two-year-old Athénaïs Mialaret,[1] with whom he had exchanged

[1] Athénaïs was born on 19 October 1826 in Montauban.

letters since October the previous year. The fifty-year-old historian immediately adored her. They courted through letters, earnest conversations, and long walks across the city and were married in a civil ceremony on 12 March 1849, just four months after they met. Mickiewicz and the popular poet Béranger[2] were witnesses for the bride while Edgar Quinet and Hector Poret ("Poinsot's heir") seconded the groom. Conspicuously absent were Adèle and Alfred Dumesnil, who disapproved.

Michelet's second marriage was an adventure as poignant and eccentric as the intimacy of love and death that dominated his formative years. Engulfed in an agitated passion for Athénaïs, he filled the *Journal* with details of their intellectual and physical intimacies. Through their mutual study of natural science, he rediscovered the world around him and celebrated its eternal powers. He was almost fifty-two when his son Lazarus was born. The couple had difficulty conceiving a child: Athénaïs had gynecological problems, and her husband's passion only aggravated her frigidity. To their joy, on 2 July 1850, a boy was born, Yves-Jean-Lazare, named after the Republican general Lazare Hoche (1768–97), who performed brilliantly during the Revolution of 1789. Michelet's infant represented the "devout hope to awaken the nations." But the child died three weeks later, on 24 August, just three days after his father's birthday.

The *Journal* did not record his intense grief: His *individual* pain was automatically *generalized* as the historian's indignation. Instead of pondering the parents' bereavement, he bemoaned the fact that Athénaïs had taken refuge in Catholic custom and insisted that the infant be baptized. The death of Lazarus, however, did not shake the Christ-like ambitions of this militant anticlerical.

Michelet did not write about the death until he could give his son's corpse a proper burial, one week after the official Christian ceremonies. He was able to undo his wife's work, as it were, by moving his father's remains to a permanent grave that it would occupy with the baby. The historian then reviewed his recent bereavement as he contemplated his father unearthed.

---

2 Pierre-Jean Béranger (1780–1857) was considered France's national bard for his lighthearted songs and political satires.

31 *August 1850, Saturday*
(*Day of my father's exhumation. Upon returning home,* 10:00 a.m.)
On 24 August, my little Yves-Jean-Lazarc died, the day of Saint-Barthelemy, the day preceding Saint-Louis day. His sickness declared itself on the twenty-first. The twenty-second, M. Blache,[3] son-in-law of M. Guersaut, came to see him; neither of them guessed.

The twenty-fourth, a double wound. My wife expressed her desire to baptize the child. I obeyed immediately. I quickly did it. If the child had died before the priest arrived, the mother's troubled heart might have attributed the child's death to the lack of religious ceremony or might have doubted if he would be saved. The opposite happened. Once the ceremony was finished, she experienced a reverse of feeling; she almost regretted it. As for me, however bitter this act that isolated me from my son, I was obligated to follow my wife's desire under those circumstances. I feel I have fulfilled a duty.

I took a leave of absence from teaching for two weeks and shut myself up with her. Except for that dark moment, she was extraordinary in heart and in reason, always ready to rise to lofty thoughts, even during the very moments of acute grief.

The plaster mold of the death mask, which finally arrived on the twenty-ninth, renewed my grief. I found the mask magnificent, touching to the highest degree. It showed the movement of a blind child and a child of genius who strives toward the light: "Light, O God, still more light!"[4]

Today, Saturday, 31 August, at 9:00 a.m., exhumation of my father at the Père-Lachaise. I had the coffin opened. I glimpsed his sacred remains with powerful constriction of the heart. Except for his head, which was completely unrecognizable (neither corpse nor skeleton),

3 The doctor.
4 These are the reputed final words of the dying Goethe (1749–1832), which Michelet quotes in *The Bird* (1856) to express nature's aspiration toward spiritual existence.

his flesh had become mummified. This proved the sobriety of his life, the pure and healthy state of his flesh, at the very last moment.

–A double exhumation further ratified death's wisdom. Michelet ignored Furcy's decomposed head and idealized the body. On 11 September 1850, after a vacation in the Fontainebleau forest, he accorded the corpses their final rest: "Exhumation and inhumation of my father and my son. Nothing moved me more deeply than to see that poor little coffin protected by the man who would have loved him so." The historian rejoiced as if his father were alive to nurture the helpless infant. The permanent tomb housed a family, reunited and purified. Three generations of Michelets faced death in perfect harmony.

After Louis-Napoleon's *coup d'état* of 2 December 1851, Michelet would no longer serve the government either as professor or at the Archives. He resigned his positions in 1852 and left Paris for Nantes where he sought respite with his young wife. He returned to Paris in 1853 and, henceforth, earned his livelihood only through his writings. He continued his *History of France* and launched a series of natural histories, *The Bird* (1856), *The Insect* (1857), *The Sea* (1861), and *The Mountain* (1868) which became best sellers. He expected these poetic, scientific, and religious essays to convert readers to a non-Christian faith in an essentially benign universe where personal immortality was guaranteed by nature. Other books of popular education, such as *Love* (1858), *Woman* (1859), *The Witch* (1862), *The Bible of Humanity* (1864), and *Our Sons* (1869), reinforced the message. His personal religion had its science, history, sociology, psychology, and pedagogy. All these books glorified the author's renewed passion for life and love, his reverence for women, the common people, and the family. His ultimate goal, in his phrase, was to "regenerate the human race."

The old historian's production only increased. By 1868 he had finished his *History of France*; his evocations of the Middle Ages, the

Renaissance, the Reformation, and the Enlightenment are its most durable masterpieces. He then reviewed and completed his autobiography in the 1869 preface to the seventeen-volume set in which he justified himself as an "artist-historian."[5] He wrote three volumes of a *History of the Nineteenth Century* (the story of Napoleon I), the last of which appeared posthumously. Michelet died in Hyères, in the South of France, exactly fifty-nine years after his mother's death, 9 February 1874.

5 English translation published in Kaplan, *Michelet's Poetic Vision*, pp. 143–68.

Epilogue
Marriage with Mother Earth

– I felt her very plainly, caressing and compassionate, warming her wounded child. On the outside? Inside as well. For she penetrated me through with her vivifying spirits, entered me and blended herself with me, infusing me with her soul. The identification between us became complete. I no longer differentiated myself from her. *The Mountain* (1868) –

—MICHELET NEVER gave up his primitive yearning to return to the womb. His wishes to die and to be reborn underlie his books on nature—first conceived during Mme Dumesnil's fatal illness and then urged to literary expression by his second wife, Athénaïs. These four essays traced his conversion to a natural religion and exhilarated readers in turn; they sold amazingly well and allowed the historian, for the first time in his life, a measure of financial security. The historian had in fact formulated his natural philosophy before he inaugurated the series, when he underwent mud bath treatments at Acqui, Italy, from 5 to 28 June 1854. The *Journal* entries of those dates brought his deepest subconscious strivings to the surface. Fourteen years later, *The Mountain* transmitted his experiences to the public.

Michelet had become severely depressed and physically ill after he left Paris in 1852, and his energetic wife attended him, organized his routine, and revived his passion for living. But he did not recuperate fully until 1854, after the hot mud therapy he received at a health resort in the Piedmont region of Italy. The small town of Acqui was the former Roman settlement of Aquae Statiellae, whose springs brought Michelet into direct contact with Mother Earth. It was almost a complete psychoanalytic regression when his imagination took over. He was healed and reborn by surrendering to Nature's womb.

Death, rebirth, marriage, and incest became one in this extraordinary event. Chapter 9 of *La Montagne* (part I)—which I here translate in its entirety—conveys Michelet's full range: dramatic autobiography; vivid descriptions of landscape and its history; animistic, quasi-scientific, and philosophical speculations; social commentary; and the author's analysis of his own mind. This sensuous visionary accepted his symbolic death and resurrection as literally true.

THE BOLLENTE AT ACQUI

"Work is my god. It preserves the world." As for me, work has truly preserved me. Thanks to work, my life has passed quite smoothly, has always maintained itself while increasing its productive energy. Except for one accident when I was about thirty years old,[1] I suspected nothing of the body's woes.

Confined within history, as I constructed my gigantic pyramid, only rarely did I gaze toward Nature, and quite late in life. Nature herself had to warn me, prove to me that I could not safely stay distant. My heart touched, guided by beloved care, one morning I found myself plunged into the life sciences. Not as a curious amusement seeker but as an imperiled voyager aboard a fragile skiff, who seeks to see through the unpredictable waves. It was quite helpful. Such passionate interest gave me a sort of second sight. It magnified my attention and at least allowed me to seize some vivid glimpses of things.

Reassured in one area, in the other I was afflicted. I was distressed, surprised (I almost said indignant) to find that I fell ill in 1853. The world gripped me for the first time. I languished at Nervi, near Genoa. That magnificent nook of the Apennines enveloped me. I was protected by the Italian sun, the light air, and the basaltic ledge where I would drag myself around noon. On that arid coast, I consumed myself in rest, a companion of the lizard. For a person whose soul remains complete, action is a growing, demanding, tyrannical necessity. It may be that the idler, who doesn't really live, or who has lived excessively, can depart more easily when his soul is thrown to the winds. But the person who is stopped while racing at full speed feels the blow quite differently. I was dying, although filled with life, with ideas, studies, and projects, powerful works that I had imagined or already begun. History, my lofty responsibility, made its claim and lamented that I could not complete it. Nature was protesting. Through science and marital happiness I had caught a glimpse of her. By what savage spite, while opening her breast to me, did she suddenly push me away? What a violent irony to say while shat-

1 Michelet alludes to the near-fatal pneumonia he contracted in November 1826; see above entry of 20 October 1839 and note 44 (chap. 2).

tering me: "Live and continue to enjoy life!"

Italy is still the country of great doctors. Their infallible oracle imposed an extreme remedy upon me. This was their sentence: "He should return to the earth. Buried under the scorching earth, he will live again."

The health-giving and funereal town, where people are buried, was Acqui, in the Monferrat district, a meager and wild little region that would have remained unknown had it not been for its strategic location and the wars in which so many perished to secure the portal of the Alps. The region itself is composed of iron, sulfur, and flint. A few scanty woods on the outskirts, and small vineyards that produce a warm, white wine that smells of flint. Through the valley flows the Bormida—a river? stream?—that doesn't lack water, but its waterfalls and abrupt leaps make it antisocial and inhospitable like its sister rivers of the Piedmont. Those watercourses which are put to such little use, on which boats never appear, seem sad and violent. The animals as well, it seems. I once saw a small ox, which looked suspiciously at me, leap forward for no reason and impale a horse with its horns.

The remains of a Roman aqueduct decorate and ennoble the valley. The ruins still stand on empty land covered by water during certain seasons. One day they will disappear under the sudden fury of waters from the Bormida and will abandon this place to its monotony.

Hot springs flourish on the two banks. The town is on the left, with its beautiful renowned spring, the Bollente. Its huge bubbles flow, transparent but strongly impregnated with sulfur. The water flows, or rather it shoots, with a pressure that suggests the height from which it comes, the rich depths at their origin. In the old days, the Roman aqueduct received these waters and carried them above the river to the baths on the other bank. Neglected now, in the Jewish section, they endure the fate of the town, which was formerly a sovereign bishopric but is now sparsely populated. However, the town is interesting, with its noble belt of impressive plane trees which surround one side and which themselves become increasingly barren as they ascend the bank of the denuded Bormida.

The right bank houses the great mystery. The earth is completely honeycombed and the hills deeply eroded with hot springs. In fact, the secret is that the mountain dies; by incessantly sifting its waters, it destroys itself in the process. Three centuries ago, the Roman baths had been swallowed up in a collapse. Now the same process occurs and will cause it to happen again. After the cave-in, the entire region was seen to be boiling. Before any building could be erected, they had to enclose and block up innumerable tiny springs. The waters became silent but remained alive underground. They made the earth vibrant. In the small groves around the baths, at the fountain where one drinks the water cold, in the hills, and everywhere —you feel as if someone, mistakenly buried, fidgets and shudders under your feet.

The baths are a kind of cloister with living quarters made up of three sides. The fourth, with a little garden and shrubs, forms an open entrance. The poor are housed at a distance, completely separated from the paying boarders. Forty years ago that separation did not exist. It is regrettable in one respect. If we lived closer to their affliction I believe we would be less frivolous. Willingly or not, we would become more mindful of our common human fate. Our venerable director, Chevalier Garrone, was quite proud that he himself checked the food they received. We were moved to see this worthy soldier, quite tall, return each morning with his buttonhole decorated with the spoon he used to test their food: noble insignia of charity.

Even if the poor were well fed, their lodgings, on the contrary, were gloomy and cramped. The narrow and bare courtyards were treeless and without shade in that scorching climate. We were told, nevertheless, that they were healed more quickly and in greater number than the rich patients. Their orderly and sober life was the reason. That expression impressed me: "They were healed." It recognizes their true right: the water, the springs, belonged to them. Nature made them for those who are able to recover.

I said to myself: "Ah! If instead of that cramped dwelling, there were a double amphitheater, a huge hospitable double pool, along the two banks of this river, a welcoming place for entire peoples, it could become a center for the future brotherhood of the Italian nations. Here Italy, that great invalid, could be cured of her pervasive sickness, the spirit of isolation and divorce!" (I wrote this in 1854.)

The baths are secondary, as is the cold water the patients drink. The main point of this treatment is the very hot mud in which you are buried.

It is not dirty mud. Its base is silica and crushed pebbles reduced to finest powder. A mixture of sulfur and iron gives it a blackish tint. In the narrow lake in which this silt lies concentrated, I admired the energetic effort of the waters which, after preparing it and sifting it in the mountain, then coagulating it, struggle against their own labor, striving to pierce the earth's opacity, and upheave the mud with slight quakings of the earth, piercing through in little jets of mud, like microscopic volcanoes. One jet may be only air bubbles, but another, permanent one shows the continuous presence of a stream that, blocked elsewhere, after immense friction has successfully conquered and obtained what it seemed to desire: the effort of these little souls delighted to see the sun.

I fixed a serious gaze on that black, living earth. I said to her: "Beloved Mother of all! We are one. I come from you, and I return to you. But frankly, then, tell me your secret. What are you doing in your dark depths, from where do you send me that warm, powerful, rejuvenating soul, that soul which wants to make me live again? What are you doing there?" She answered: "What you see. What I do is before your eyes."

She spoke clearly, rather softly, but with a gentle voice, distinctly maternal.

Her mysteries are exaggerated. Her work is simple and obvious in those places where she works, as it were, in the sunlight.

I arrived on 5 June, still quite weak.[2] I had fainted as I left the carriage. Then I slept for twelve hours straight and awoke somewhat recovered. We had a beautiful bedroom with a terrace that opened on the limited but pleasant view of a little wood, crossed by rather attractive arbors, which you saw at the entrance. The vegetation was scanty, and the strong odor of sulfur was everywhere.

Powerful smell of life. The water in some of the neighboring springs intoxicates you as much as wine. The intoxication of the air and waters stimulates and awakens the senses, well before it restores your strength. You forget that you are ill. My spark returned on the ninth. Already I felt alive.

The night was a fairylike scene. The atmosphere of sulfur and love intoxicated our fireflies. Nimbler than those of the North, these winged creatures, in their burning dances, glittered in the dim darkness of the little wood, which seemed all the darker as background to those diamond showers. Their flames changed infinitely, sparkling at their meetings, sometimes pale and faint from desire or weariness.

These insects are not the only ones. In the absence of noisy pleasures, Nature acts even more, and with little mystery, in this deeply serious place where there exists true, infinitely painful suffering. Blind human fireflies reach out to each other for a moment, flutter about, and then withdraw without remembering. Our life was more concentrated and held us rather apart. During the evenings we preferred to walk on the banks of the Bormida, illumined by a beautiful

2 The following sections condense the *Journal* entries of 5–28 June 1854 (vol. 2, pp. 262–74).

sunset, or climb the hill by the former Roman road. From there the town on the opposite bank was revealed. You see the meanders of the river. To one side you can even catch a glimpse of the Viso, so elevated, which crowns the landscape without lending it grandeur. Everything disappears on the other side of the hill, and you see nothing but the narrow, rugged valley of the stream, the Ravanesco, and, far away, the cemetery and some deserted houses.

One day, on that hill, on a lovely day of Corpus-Christi, we encountered a sorrowful funeral procession that had been organized hastily and late. Burials here are quite brief, so as not to depress the patients, especially the convalescents with their petty diversions. A young man was being buried who, like them, had forgotten why he had come. That unexpected funeral, during a beautiful time of year, made me reflect, penetrated as I was with the strong, gentle feeling of the Italian summer, fate, death, and the Alps. All these great and lofty ideas said that only love could cure all the empty seductions of the world. Love is life's measure, its limit. With its tender solicitude, love is wisdom itself.

On 19 June, having been well prepared, I was finally buried, but only up to the waist. In my magnificent coffin of white marble, I received the first application of black, oily mud. However, it hardly soiled me, for it was essentially sand. Alongside, another marble bath receives you afterward and cleans you instantly.

Signor Tomasini, the *fangarolo* who applied the mud to my body, was an intelligent, pleasant, and clever man. He was even educated and had completed the philosophy class. We talked. He told me that in the winter he hunted for his living, snaring small birds, for there was no other game. He owned a little land, worth about twenty-five thousand francs. One of his sons was to inherit it. But he wanted the other to become a notary. He did not regret his own fate. He only worried about rivalry with the senior *fangaroli*, whose positions were until now hereditary. They hated him as a newcomer since he had worked there for only twenty years.

On 20 June the earth encroached further upon me, to my stomach, covering me almost completely. On the twenty-first I disappeared. Only my face remained free to let me breathe. I could then appreciate my burier's talent. He was a skilled sculptor in the Egyptian style. I found myself (except the face) completely and beautifully molded in this funereal clothing. I might already believe myself a citizen of the dark kingdom.

Strange disguise. Yet nothing that should be too surprising. Will I not someday be placed in the earth, probably in a few years? There is little difference between this grave and that one. Our birthplace, the earth, where our race was born, is it not as well the birthplace from which we are reborn? Let us hope so. We are in good hands.

At first I felt only a vague well-being. State very much like dreaming. After several experiences, I distinguished between the successive stages, which were different from each other.

During the first quarter-hour, complete peace. The mind, still free, observed itself. I questioned myself, my sickness and its cause. I blamed only myself and my badly regulated will, my excessive efforts to revive the life of humankind all by myself. The dead with whom I have conversed for so long enticed me and wanted me on the other shore. Nature still holds me and wants me to remain on this one.

During the second quarter-hour, her power increased. Thinking disappeared in my deep absorption. The only idea retained was that of *terra mater* [Mother Earth]. I felt her very plainly, caressing and compassionate, warming her wounded child. On the outside? Inside as well. For she penetrated me through with her vivifying spirits, entered me and blended herself with me, infusing me with her soul. The identification between us became complete. I no longer differentiated myself from her.

From this point to the last quarter-hour, that part of me she did not cover—my face—, the part that remained free, bothered me. The buried body was happy, and it was I. The unburied head protested and was no longer I. At least that is how it seemed. So complete was the marriage—and more than a marriage—between the Earth and me! One might say an *exchange of nature.*[3] I was Earth, and she was man. She had taken my infirmity, my sin, upon herself. As for me, in becoming Earth, I had taken her life, her warmth, her youth.

Years, labors, grief, everything remained at the bottom of my marble coffin. I was renewed. When I emerged, my body was covered by some sort of oily glow. It was a certain organic element whose nature we do not know, different from minerals. It gives the impression of a living contact, of having communicated with the invisible soul and the benevolent warmth it then transmits.

Nature, whom I had forgotten for the fierce work that so blindly evaded happiness, did not hold it too much against me. With infinite gentleness she had again opened her arms and was waiting for me. She had increased my life and power. I said to myself: May I deserve it, drink from her streams, and with a more fertile heart enter into her sacred unity!

The Bird, The Sea, The Insect were born of this experience, as was *The Renaissance,* and the book which made them, and which makes everything: *Love.*[4]

3 Michelet's italics (in French, *un échange de nature*).

4 Michelet resumed his historical epic at *The Renaissance,* published in February 1855. His first book on marriage, *Love,* appeared in November 1858, followed by *Woman* in November 1859.

References

These are basic background readings and sources used in the preparation of *Mother Death*. Interested readers will find exhaustive bibliographies in several of the works noted below. Easy access to Michelet's historical context can be found in J. L. Talmon, *Romanticism and Revolt: Europe 1815–1849* (New York: Harcourt, Brace, World, 1967), and Donald G. Charlton, *Secular Religions in France, 1815–1870* (London: Oxford University Press, 1963).

Introduction

From the numerous good books related to death I would choose: Philippe Ariès, *The Hour of Our Death* (New York: Alfred Knopf, 1981); Jacques Choron, *Death and Western Thought* (New York: Collier Books, 1963); Geoffrey Gorer, *Death, Grief, and Mourning in Contemporary Britain* (Garden City, N.J.: Doubleday, 1965); Elizabeth Kübler-Ross, *On Death and Dying* (New York: Macmillan, 1969); Ernest Becker, *The Denial of Death* (New York: Free Press, 1973).

Since Sigmund Freud's classic paper "Mourning and Melancholia" (1917), psychoanalysts have studied grieving with great insight. See Elliot Jaques, "Death and the Mid-Life Crisis," *International Journal of Psychoanalysis* 46 (1965): 502–14. The significant theories are critically reviewed in John Bowlby's *Attachment and Loss: Attachment*, vol. 1 (New York: Basic Books, 1969); *Separation: Anxiety and Anger*, vol. 2 (Basic Books, 1973); and *Loss: Sadness and Depression* (Basic Books, 1980). See also Avery D. Weisman, *On Dying and Denying* (New York: Behavioral Publications, 1972). Articles that summarize the issues: John Bowlby, "Processes of Mourning," *Int. Journ. Psychoan.* 42 (1961): 317–40; Lorraine Siggins, "Mourning: A Critical Survey of the Literature," *Int. Journ. Psychoan.* 47 (1966): 14–25. The most suggestive anthology is *Death and Dying: Challenge and Change* (Reading, Mass.: Addison-Wesley, 1978).

A superb introduction to Michelet has recently appeared: Oscar A. Haac, *Jules Michelet* (Boston: Twayne Publishers, 1982), which contains the most useful bibliography. In French the fundamental biography remains Gabriel Monod, *Jules Michelet: Etudes sur sa vie et ses oeuvres* (Paris: Hachette, 1905) and *La Vie et pensée de J. M. (1798–1852)* (Paris: Libraire Champion, 1923; available in Slatkine reprints). I have also used with caution the memoir of a close friend of the Michelet family, Eugène Noël, *Michelet et ses enfants* (Paris: Maurice Dreyfous, 1878), which contains anecdotes and personal letters. *Lettres inédites* (1841–1871), ed. Paul Sirven (Paris:

Presses Universitaires de France, 1924) was another important source. The thesis of Paul Viallaneix, *La Voie royale* (Paris: Delagrave, 1959; Flammarion, 1971), is a foundation for Michelet studies as is Oscar Haac, *Les Principes inspirateurs de Michelet* (Paris: Presses Universitaires de France, 1951). For the second half of Michelet's life, see Linda Orr, *Jules Michelet: Nature, History, and Language* (Ithaca, N.Y.: Cornell University Press, 1976); her excellent chapter 7, "A Strange Sexuality," fully documents the incest themes traced in these *Journals*. And Edward K. Kaplan, *Michelet's Poetic Vision: A Romantic Philosophy of Nature, Man, and Woman* (Amherst: University of Massachusetts Press, 1977) studies the quasi-scientific and philosophical system and Michelet's self-portrait as androgynous man of genius; on pp. 107–10 I analyze Michelet's union with Mother Earth. See the Epilogue of the present book for my translation of the entire chapter from *The Mountain*.

My critical editions of *L'Oiseau* (*The Bird*) and *L'Insecte* (*The Insect*) will comprise volume 17 of the *Oeuvres complètes*, now in press at Flammarion, Paris.

The themes relating to death have been treated especially well by the following: Roland Barthes, *Michelet par lui-même* (Paris: Le Seuil, 1954; 1965); Michel Crouzet, "Michelet, les morts et l'année 1842," *Annales*, January–February 1976, pp. 182–96; Lionel Gossman, "The Go-between: Jules Michelet, 1798–1874," *MLN* 89 (1974): 503–41; Frank E. Manuel, "Michelet and the Philosophy of History," *Clio* 6, 2 (winter 1977): 149–65; Jacques Seebacher, "Le Côté de la mort, ou l'histoire comme clinique," *Revue d'histoire littéraire de la France* 74 (September–October 1974): 810–23.

Michelet's relationships with women, and the role of females in his works, have been surveyed by Jeanne Calo, *La Création de la femme chez Michelet* (Paris: Nizet, 1975), while a more focused psychoanalytical study is Thérèse Moreau, *Le Sang de l'histoire. Michelet, l'histoire et l'idée de la femme au XIXe siècle* (Paris: Flammarion, 1982).

Paul Viallaneix has traced a history of the *Journal* in his editions of *Ecrits de jeunesse* (Paris: Gallimard, 1959), pp. 11–39, and *Journal*, vol. 1 (Gallimard, 1959), pp. 7–32. Viallaneix quotes the entry of 1 November 1864 in *Journal*, 1:17, but it does not appear in Claude Digeon's edition of vol. 3 (Gallimard, 1976).

Prologue. A Memorial to Mother and Friend

Selections from the *Memorial* are from *Ecrits de jeunesse*, pp. 214–17. Michelet's translation of the passage from Seneca, p. 398, n. 2.

1 THE DEATH OF MY DEAREST FRIEND

Selections from *Ecrits de jeunesse*, 1821: pp. 132–36, 141, 144, 146, 152–53, 158, 166–68.

Michelet's poem to Mme Fourcy, p. 344 in note. Monod and Viallaneix only hint that Michelet had sexual relations with her; it has been demonstrated conclusively by

A. Govindane in *Michelet cent ans après*, a special issue of *Romantisme* 10 (1975): 197–202.

Selections from *Journal*, vol. 1, 1834: pp. 116–17, 120; 1837: pp. 219–21.

Some entries of 1837 and 1838 are incorrectly dated in the Viallaneix edition. Following the catalog prepared by the staff of the Bibliothèque historique de la Ville de Paris, *Moi-Paris* (1975), which I confirmed on the manuscripts, I have changed 8 May 1834 (J. 1, p. 117) to 18 May 1834; and 18 March 1837 (J. 1, p. 220) to 18 March 1838. More important, Poinsot's exhumation did not take place in April 1837 as printed in the Viallaneix edition. The catalog *Moi-Paris* correctly dates it 25 April 1838 and I have confirmed text and date on the original manuscript page (Papiers Michelet. Voyages III, f° 10) and at the Père-Lachaise. My thanks to Mme Emilie Méneses of the cemetery archives for helping me verify this and other facts.

For a history of the Père-Lachaise cemetery and all the rules and regulations operating in Michelet's time see F.-T. Salomon, *Le Père-Lachaise, Recueil général et alphabétique de concessions perpétuelles* (Paris: Chez l'auteur, Boulevard de Strasbourg, 1855). This book reminded me that French cemeteries have two types of tombs, permanent and temporary. Michelet's exhumations were not as extraordinary as I had first assumed. My thanks to Mlle Odile Sanson of the Bibliothèque historique de la Ville de Paris for this important source.

Michelet's letters of June 1837 to Pauline are in notes of *Journal* 1, pp. 772–74, as is most of their correspondence.

2 MY WIFE'S DEATH

Selections from *Journal* 1, 1839: pp. 289, 305–10, 311–18, 324–25; 1840: pp. 328–29; 1841: pp. 357–63.

Pauline's epitaph was first published in Noël (1878), p. 64, reproduced in Monod (1905), p. 81, and *Journal* 1:803, note. The epitaph contains a quotation from Horace preceded by a verse from Psalm 40. Noël describes Bishop Allou's exhumation of Bossuet on p. 58 of his book. For Gasparin's letter to Michelet on Joan of Arc, see Viallaneix, *La Voie royale* (1971), p. 362.

3 THE DEATH OF MY WHITE ANGEL

Selections from *Journal* 1, 1842: pp. 377–81, 384–85, 398–407, 411–12, 478. 1843: pp. 516–17. 1845: pp. 598–99.

Michelet's letter to Dumesnil in Monod (1905), pp. 104–5. Mme Dumesnil's letter to Alfred about the historian's first visit in *Journal* 1:804, note to 24 May 1840. Alfred's letter of June 1840 to Eugène Noël, written soon after he and his mother moved to the rue des Postes, in Noël (1878), pp. 68–74. The Noël-Dumesnil correspondence, most of it still unpublished, is conserved at the Bibliothèque historique de la Ville de Paris. See Monod, *Vie et pensée* (1923), "La Crise de 1840 à 1842," pp. 55–80.

The name of Tony Toullion was misprinted as "Touillon" in *Journal* 1. The name of one of his teachers, Amaury-Duval, was misprinted in the entry of 25 July 1839.

4 MY FATHER'S DEATH

Selections from *Journal* 1, 1845: pp. 621–22, 623; 1846: pp. 653–59; 1847: pp. 678–79. For detailed analyses of these entries, see E. K. Kaplan, "Michelet's Revolutionary Symbolism: From Hermeneutics to Politics," *French Review* 40, 5(April 1977): 713–23.

5 EXHUMATION AND REBURIAL OF MY FATHER AND MY SON

Selections from *Journal* 2, 1850: pp. 123, 131.

EPILOGUE. MARRIAGE WITH MOTHER EARTH.

My translation is based on the first edition, *La Montagne* (Paris: Librarie internationale. Lacroix et Verboeckhoven, 1868). A complete translation of *The Mountain* by W. H. Davenport Adams, with illustrations by Percival Skelton, was published by T. Nelson and Sons, London, in 1872. The other books on nature also appeared in charming Victorian illustrated editions. All of them should be retranslated and republished.

Index